*Walking with
Windows of Light*

Walking with Windows of Light

A Diary of My Early Years
with Swami Chinmayananda

Neeru Mehta

Woodstock, New York, USA

IN HONOR OF HIS 100TH BIRTHDAY

Published by: Namah Inc.
PO Box 1064
Woodstock, NY 12498
www.walkingwithwindowsoflight.com
www.namahom.org

Editorial Team: Deborah Seroff, Poonam Patni, Rajpriya & Shubhraji

Book Design & Production: Ann Lowe
Cover Design: Ann Lowe

First Edition

Copyright 2016 © by Neeru Mehta & Namah Inc.

All rights reserved. No part of this publication, except for brief quotations embodied in reviews or for other noncommercial uses permitted by copyright law, may be reproduced, stored in retrieval systems, distributed, or transmitted in any form or by any means—electronic, mechanical, photocopying, recording, or otherwise—without written permission of the publisher.

Printed in the United States of America by CreateSpace

Neeru Mehta.
   Walking With Windows Of Light
   a diary of my early years with Swami Chinmayananda
   ISBN 978-0-9912578-4-3 (paperback)

Summary: A personal diary of a spiritual seeker. Tracking the early years of the devotee and her interactions with her guru or teacher. - Publisher.

1. Spirituality 2. Self-realization 3. Personal Diary 4. Vedanta

Dedicated to my Guru,
Pujya H. H. Swami Chinmayananda (1916–1993),
The light in my life.

"When the right time comes for the seeker to embark on the path the teacher himself appears. It is just like a flowering plant that is found by the bee looking for nectar."

–Swami Chinmayananda

Acknowledgments

*M*y prostrations to the great masters Swami Akhandanandaji Maharaj, Sri Ma Anandamayi, Sri Nisargadatta Maharaj and Dada Bhagavan who shone their blazing loving light into the window of my heart.

A very special thanks to Deborah Seroff, Woodstock, NY, USA, for the many months she spent arranging the material for this book, shaping it so lovingly, and for all her editing work.

Thank you Ann Lowe for your generous time and creativity in designing this book. Your having visited Swami Chinmayanandaji's ashram in Sidhabari, India, makes it even more special.

Thanks to:

My parents, Prem Narain and Swarnlata Tandon, who nurtured me in a loving atmosphere, allowing my spirituality to bloom.

My husband Ravindra, for his steady support, and for becoming a true devotee of Swamiji as well.

My children Shilpa, Ashish, and Shreya who grew up around the care and attention of Swamiji.

My sisters, Preeta and Rashmi, and my brother Peush for their love and support.

My brothers in law Gopal and Saurabh and my sister in law Nelu for their encouragement.

My youngest sister Shubhraji, for guiding the entire process of this book, for devoting hours over the years to make sure that we publish it during the Birth Centenary year of our Guru.

My son-in-law Primit, my daughter in law Vaidehi and my grandchildren Illisha, Ananya and Shivani, for coming into the circle of Swamiji's influence by being part of our family.

My cousin Poonam Patni, who interacted with Swamiji in Boston along with her husband Naren, and helped to complete this book with painstaking efforts, perseverance and valuable insight.

Rajpriya Bhuckory, Mauritius, who devoted many hours to proofread, offer suggestions and help to complete the manuscript.

Sanjay Misra, Dubai and Orient Links India Pvt. Limited for their generosity in donating the paper for printing this book.

Dr. V. K. Seth for his contribution towards the publication of this book.

Dominique Fung, Hong Kong, for her loving contribution towards this project.

Anjali Singh, my spiritual sister and friend, for the cover photograph and for the joy we have shared through the years of satsang and being around Swamiji.

I WOULD LIKE TO THANK MY GLOBAL SPIRITUAL FAMILY:

With deep respects to Babaji of Jageshwar, Swami Prakashananda.

With gratitude to Swami Tejomayananda.

My Chinmaya family: Smt Kusubem Patel, Capt. S. R. Yadav, Ajay Singh, Dwarak Reddy, Thangam and Chandrashekhar Varrier, K. K. Rajan, Kalidas, Dr. Sneh Chakravarthy, Dinesh Trivedi and Dr. Channa Reddy.

My heartfelt thanks to Swami Anubhavananda.

Trivedi Bapuji Sanand, Praful Amin.

In deep appreciation for Swami Vimalananada Saraswati.

Judge N. Desai, Geeta and Vinay Singh, and Jatinbhai Shah.

My longtime friends: Late Birendra Kumar, Geeta Bhargava, Dr. Harshida Thakkar, Meera and Prashant Pandya, Bella Salerno, and Pushpa and Arun Shah.

Prologue

AUGUST 3, 1998
THE FIFTH MAHASAMADHI PUJA OF
PARAM PUJYA GURUDEV SWAMI CHINMAYANANDA
EVENING SATSANG AT SIDHABARI ASHRAM

*T*HE NIGHT WAS QUIET. A gentle mountain breeze rustled through the trees. The dark monsoon clouds, which had threatened rain earlier in the day, slowly parted and the moon appeared, bathing the countryside with a silver glow. It seemed as if Nature was also paying tribute to Swami Chinmayananda today, the fifth anniversary of his *mahasamadhi* (passing away).

Later that night, I sat and watched the lamp flickering in front of Swamiji's statue in the *Mahasamadhi Mandir*. This was his final resting place. I could see the mandir from the window of my room which had been personally selected by Swamiji. It was room 124 in the Anjaneya Block, behind the majestic statue of Sri Hanumanji. From there I had a beautiful view of the Himalayas; a stunning backdrop to the Mahasamadhi Mandir. To the right as far as the eye could see was the wide expanse of the pinewood forests.

My thoughts strayed back to the evening satsang when Swami Tejomayananda, the worldwide head of the

Chinmaya Mission, joined some of Swami Chinmayananda's ardent devotees as we shared our memories of Gurudev.

As I narrated some events which revealed my Guru, Swamiji's, *kripa* (grace), various incidents from my life began playing in my mind like a film. Memories of *satsangs*, the devotional gatherings in the presence of a master, during the twenty years from 1973 to 1993, were engraved in my heart; glorious moments of my transformation at the direction of my all knowing Swamiji. I remembered the letter Swamiji wrote to me on May 30, 1991, while he was in the United States, "You publish the notes and use my stray thoughts recorded, each bit under quotation marks." Suddenly, the inspiration to record my experiences grew stronger.

Swami Chinmayananda was one of the most dynamic spiritual masters of his time. The Vedanta philosophy expounded by Swamiji may be more clearly explained if we consider the analogy of electricity. Imagine God to be the total source of electricity present in the entire universe. The guru's work is to harness the electricity that is within us just like an expert electrical engineer. He knows the laws and workings of the electrical currents (the vital prana or forces of energy).

Man uses electrical power to facilitate his daily activities without ever noticing its presence. He sees electricity manifest in various forms but is most aware of its value

Prologue

when it is unavailable, as in a faulty fuse or downed power line. Electricity is in no way less or more by its expression or by the failure of electrical equipment. In the same way, God Consciousness is the source of infinite eternal power. The Masters know this by their direct experience. They try to teach us how to value, conserve, and utilize this power to improve the quality of our lives. To the more serious seeker, the Masters teach the secret science of generating and channeling that power by various methods called *yoga*.

Truly speaking, no one can possibly describe the silent inner state of a realized master. We can only describe the most dynamic aspects of his personality by the telling of events. I strongly believe that if by reading this book even one reader becomes inspired to seek the blessings of a living master it will be by the grace of Swami Chinmayananda. It is the master alone who can unveil the light that exists in our hearts.

It is a great privilege to transcribe my diaries into a book and share my personal experiences. With Swamiji in my heart, I now bring this manuscript to you.

Another light from the window, Nisarga Dutta Maharaj

Dada Bhagwan, founder of the Akram Vigyan Movement

Introduction

August 3, 1998
Sidhabari Ashram
Rishi Pancham – holy day of tribute to the ancient masters

The following pages reveal different facets of a perfect diamond, reflecting the sparkling hues of the entire spectrum of colors. Our revered Master Swami Chinmayananda, "Swamiji", as I always called him, was a man of perfection, a *Sthithaprajna* or one who is established in the knowledge of the Self. He was a master of Vedanta, and one who lived its values. He believed in giving "maximum happiness to maximum number." Swamiji was a patriot, a freedom fighter, whose goal was no less than the discovery of the true Self.

These pages were reproduced from my diaries, which I wrote over a period of twenty years during various satsangs. The entries were originally written in Hindi and English, beginning in 1973, when I first met Swamiji, until 1993, the year of his *mahasamadhi* (passing away, when the spirit of a holy man leaves the body). Some sections containing teachings on the Upanishads and Bhagavad Geeta have not been included in this book since they have already been published by the Chinmaya Mission.

The topics covered deal with life in its myriad moods and seasons, as seen through the eyes of a Self-realized Master. Swamiji addresses the queries and concerns of householders, businessmen and seekers of Truth from different strata of society. Much of what you will be reading comes directly from Swamiji himself, in his own words.

During satsang in 1975 while in Montreal, Canada, Swamiji described the two types of Self-realized masters. The master who plunges back into the ocean of *samsara* (the endless cycle of birth and death) to help save his fellow human beings. A master who is not worried about getting his clothes wet dives back in with infinite compassion. At the same time, the other Self-realized master just sits on the shore, calling out from a distance, giving directions on how to save oneself. Swamiji belonged to the former type of compassionate masters, the one who jumped back into the ocean of samsara.

I was especially blessed during the first years of meeting Swamiji when I traveled extensively with him for *yagnas* (vedic fire ritual, can also mean spiritual discourse) and other programs which were held in Canada, Manila, London, Nairobi, and the United States. During my repeated visits to Sidhabari, Powai, Bombay, Lucknow and Allentown, Pennsylvania, there were often many blessed opportunities for being alone with Swamiji. We also had meaningful satsangs with other devotees.

The holy river Ganga in Uttarkashi had a special spiritual significance for me from our very first visit in 1973 until the 1993 visit for Swamiji's *shodasi* ceremony. This is a ritual performed sixteen days after a master's soul departs the body. According to Swamiji, I was like a *kora kagaz* (blank paper), because I didn't know much about rituals. I had never met a *mahatma* (great soul) prior to Swamiji except for a saint who once came to our house for *bhiksha* (a meal prepared as an offering to the guru) when I was fifteen years old. He gave me a personal mantra. A mantra is a chosen word or phrase that a seeker repeats to oneself in prayer, in order to purify the mind. Swamiji was gracious in allowing me to continue practicing this mantra. When I asked him if he would give me a new one, he said, "It has brought you here, you continue this mantra."

I am sure that all those who have been blessed by their own guru, and those who have not yet found a guru, will benefit by reading these recollections of mine.

A *sadguru* is like a light, full of powers. In Sanskrit *sat* means Truth, *gu* means darkness and *ru* means to remove, to counter-act. Therefore, *sadguru* is one who removes the darkness of ignorance about Truth or God. This concept is a tradition in Eastern philosophy. The guru is an institution rather than an individual personality.

In this field of self knowledge and spirituality, a good conductor of love, compassion and total acceptance automatically passes on the current of divinity from himself as the guru to the *shishya* (disciple) lighting up his heart. The brilliance and clarity of light depends upon the purity of the mind and heart of the individual disciple. The darkness and despair is lifted forever, bringing a new vision and meaning to one's life.

In 1973 I had given Swamiji my notes on select verses of an elementary Vedanta text called *Atmabodha*. After reading them, he returned the notebook to me with a written comment, "Good! I have lit a torch for you to carry on this journey. In the cave of samsara, as you walk ahead, you will see the light coming from other windows too."

Reflecting on Swamiji's words, I think 'windows' meant empty space. The light can pour in only when we are open. In moments of emptiness, whenever the disciple's ego is not present, this light of truth manifests in the consciousness.

In the coming years, many such windows did open. I had the opportunity to meet enlightened masters who blessed me on my spiritual journey. It was in 1973 that Swamiji introduced me to the great saint, Sri Ma Anandamayi (Ma signifies respected mother). That satsang will be described in the coming pages.

In 1975, Swamiji asked me to deliver some medicine to Swami Akhandanandaji Saraswati, the foremost exponent of *Srimad Bhagavatam*. This text has been called the Holy

Bible of the Hindus. He was a great saint from Vrindavan, the sacred home of Lord Krishna and one of the most holy cities of India. He blessed me and came often to my home in Bombay and Ahmedabad.

In 1978 I was fortunate to have the satsang and close contact of a self-realized *advaitin*, a scholar and practitioner of the theory of non-duality. Sri Nisarga Dutta Maharaj of Bombay was both a householder and a *gyani* (one who has attained self-realization). He was the author of the well-known book *I Am That*. Sri Dutta blessed us often with visits to our home in Bombay for bhiksha. For me, this was the fulfillment of my prayer made in Swamiji's presence, when I accompanied him to Sai Baba's temple in Shirdi.

The year 1982 was an extremely difficult period for me personally. However, while visiting Los Angeles, USA, I received the *Gyanavidhi* (Way of Knowledge) blessings from the compassionate gyani householder sage of Gujarat, Dada Bhagwan. He propagated *Akram Vigyan* and *Pratikramana* (repent and forgive), based on the Jain philosophy. This is a very helpful practice to help clear our hearts. He also came several times to our home in Ahmedabad for bhiksha and satsang, accompanied by his followers.

Swamiji has ignited the divine spark in thousands of fellow beings who are lighting various paths in the world of education, health and self-reliance. They are also spreading the message of *Sanatana Dharma*, the eternal values of life.

In 2001, on the occasion of the Golden Jubilee of the Chinmaya Mission, this garland of golden, fragrant memories of Swamiji in satsang, tied with the string of devotion, is offered to its founder and our Master, Param Pujya Priya Swami Chinmayananda.

By the grace of Sri Sadguru Swamiji may this Light within and without illumine my heart, HERE AND NOW!

•

–Neeru

December 31, 1972
Bangalore, India

*M*y family and I went on a spiritual tour of South India and visited many famous landmarks before arriving in Bangalore. It is a cosmopolitan city, the center of India's high-tech industry and is also known as the Silicon Valley of India.

We arrived at the Ashoka Hotel on New Year's Eve. A rather loud party was in full swing. The atmosphere in the room was festive and bright and was a stark contrast to the darkness I was feeling in my heart. The questions within became louder. Is this the purpose of life, to spend time in this flippant way when we know time is running out? We can never know how life will unfold for us or when we will take our last breath!

My desire to get some guidance, to meet a master who could answer all of my questions about life and satisfy my seeking mind was at its peak.

Powai, Bombay, February 1973

January 2, 1973
First Meeting
Bangalore, India

*L*ooking out of the window of my hotel room I could see the sunlight filtering through the leaves. It looked like stars sparkling on a canopy of evergreen trees. Being in Bangalore, the city of gardens, on this pleasant January afternoon was a welcome retreat from the crowded commercial city of Bombay.

My family and I had gone to Whitefield the previous day for a *darshan* (meeting) of the famous Guru Sri Satya Sai Baba. I left feeling a bit more at peace, but I still hadn't found the Truth I had been searching for.

I decided to write a letter to Satya Sai Baba, requesting guidance. Little did I know that I would get my answer within the hour and I definitely didn't expect it to arrive the way it did!

My children, Shilpa and Ashish, had gone with my husband Ravindra for a swim in the pool. This gave me some free time to visit my husband's niece, who was also staying at the hotel on another floor. She was not well and I thought a visit might lift her spirits.

The elevator was temporarily out of service, but this difficulty turned out to be a boon. As I walked down the stairs, I noticed a lot of slippers and shoes in front of a door. Some political V.I.P. or some religious dignitary must have been visiting. I then came across two middle-aged ladies climbing the same staircase and carrying flowers. I didn't hesitate to ask them, "Please, excuse me, do you know who is visiting here, staying in this room?" They answered, "Swami Chinmayananda. Would you like to come with us?" My heart was full of gratitude for these two angels. I later learned they were Mrs. Dwarak Reddy and Mrs. Indira Reddy from Chittoor. Overwhelmed with excitement I asked the women, "Can I come with you?" They agreed happily and took me to the suite where Swamiji was staying. I had a strong feeling that my answer had just arrived in the form of Swamiji.

We sat with approximately twenty-five other visitors in the living room of the large suite. Swamiji was in an adjoining room in a closed door meeting with some members of the Chinmaya Mission Organization from Bangalore and Central Chinmaya Mission Trust from Bombay. Swamiji later told me this was the first time he had decided to stay in a hotel in India. He had done this in order to avoid differences of opinions among his devotees regarding the place of his stay. He wanted all to feel equally important and united for the First National Geeta Gyana Yagna to be held in Bangalore in May, 1973.

I quietly waited almost an hour and a half for what was

about to change my life forever. I was so full of anticipation about meeting Swamiji that I started thinking about the sudden demise of my father, Prem Narain Tandon, at the young age of fifty-one. I sat wondering about the nature of death and the purpose of life.

I had originally heard about Swamiji from Dr. N.R. Desai, a family friend and the brother of Morarji Desai, a former Prime Minister of India. He had given me a text on Vedanta called the *Kathopanishad* with commentary written by Swami Chinmayananda.

In April of 1972, seated in the last row of the Oval Maidan in Bombay, I had the opportunity to hear Swamiji give a discourse. He was speaking on the Geeta, chapter XVIII. I immediately purchased the entire set of his commentaries on the Bhagavad Geeta and began regularly reading a few verses at a time. I had just completed reading all eighteen chapters when I felt an overwhelming desire to meet this enlightened master who so authoritatively roared Vedanta. It is that knowledge of the true Self, which alone can remove all sorrows permanently.

As I sat waiting in this hotel suite in Bangalore, I began to get anxious about the time. I had previously committed to a business dinner with my husband and some of our colleagues at eight o'clock that night. I was hoping that Swamiji would come out before I had to leave.

Some of the others, also patiently waiting to meet this great Master, started singing *bhajans* (spiritual songs), which inspired me to sing as well. Suddenly, I remembered a childhood bhajan called *Jai Jai Pita Paramanand Data* which I sang as a child with my maternal grandfather, Rai Bahadur Madan Mohan Seth. My grandfather had a great influence on me during my youth. He was a chief justice during the British Raj and was conferred the honorable title of Rai Bahadur. He was also the President of All India Arya Samaj, a religious and social reform order initiated by Swami Dayanand Saraswati.

Although we were all strangers in that room, I didn't feel the slightest bit uncomfortable in singing. With exactly one minute remaining before I had to leave, Swamiji suddenly came striding into the room. He was smiling, alert and radiated energy. We all touched his feet as he blessed us. I was a little surprised to see a Swami laughing and joking.

Swamiji was tall and majestic. He was clad in a crisp lungi-style, ochre-colored *dhoti* (a piece of cloth worn by men and women, wrapped around the waist) and a long *kurta* (tunic). He wore his hair slightly long and had a gold wristwatch on his right hand. He stood erect and walked briskly in his wooden *khadaus* (sandals).

Swamiji was full of life. He was smiling as he looked around the room at all of his devotees, who stood up, as soon he entered the room. The atmosphere was charged with a bright, vibrant, warm energy. Swamiji spoke at length about his tours in the United States and the Middle East, from which he had recently returned.

I did *namaskaram*, a greeting done with folded palms which is a sign of reverence. Speaking to Swamiji, I asked if he might answer some questions for me. His reply, "All right, you come tomorrow morning at 8 a.m." was like music to my ears.

Later I wrote down my questions in case my nerves got the better of me while speaking to this powerful Master. I didn't want to waste one minute of this precious opportunity.

I had no idea that one should take some offering when going to meet a saint or a guru. I would have gone empty handed but as it turned out, my husband and I received many incense sticks and sandalwood garlands as gifts that night. The Lord kindly provided them to us, so that I could take them with me, as an offering to Swamiji the following morning.

January 3, 1973

*T*HIS WAS AN AUSPICIOUS DAY for me as it was Shilpa's birthday and my first personal meeting with a master. I took her and Ashish with me to meet Swamiji. Ravindra felt he had had enough of all the spiritual searching, so he decided not to accompany us.

I was very excited about coming face to face with a realized master; he had sparked within me that which had been lying dormant. He had inspired me to seek that "something", some goal, which is higher than day-to-day life. And so it happened that I found myself in the presence of the revered Swami Chinmayananda. I handed him, in the form of a letter, the questions I had written down the night before. That letter and his reply are as follows:

Most Respected Swamiji,

You said (referring to his commentary on *Kathopanishad*) that people do not work with enthusiasm. Maybe they do not have the vision of the ultimate reality, the all-pervading Consciousness. But how does working this way affect our daily lives here on this earth? Unless the soul gets the opportunity to hear the clear inner voice of the Lord within, or has a glimpse of the ultimate reality which is full of bliss, how can he or she strive for it? If the soul can get a small definite experience only then will the individual be motivated to strive with all his energies towards this ultimate reality. One has to get some taste of that joyful knowledge that is within one's heart.

The question is, how does one get that opportunity, or the taste of THAT? What is the ultimate goal of our lives? Just this day-to-day living is so meaningless when we know that all this is transitory and not permanent. If this cycle of life and death continues until the soul reaches or merges in THAT, *Paramatma* or the Supreme Being, why did God or Consciousness create these different individuals in the first place? When all of us have a part of that great Consciousness in us what is the ultimate aim of trying to merge again into the Source? Why have we fallen away from THAT — the eternal source of light?

One has to live one's life in the best possible way given the type of circumstances in which one finds oneself. In this lifetime am I in this particular position due to His Grace? What are my duties as an individual, wife, mother, and member of society? What can I do, and in what manner, so that I try to walk on the right path leading me to my liberation? I don't know, I cannot express myself clearly.

Am I worthy of making this request, for you to become my sadguru? I hope I am not too presumptuous. If I am not worthy, what should I do until I become worthy?

Some of my faults I know, and some are unknown. What is the best way that I can make my life more meaningful and improve my 'self'?

Neeru
OM HARI OM

JANUARY 3, 1973
SWAMIJI'S VERBAL RESPONSE
[My thoughts are in parenthesis.]

"WHEN THE RIGHT TIME COMES for the seeker to embark on the path the teacher himself appears. It is just like a flowering plant that is found by the bee looking for nectar. As you mature, your excitement in material things and dissipation of mental energy is reduced. Then this energy can be conserved for meditation and building up equanimity.

"First a person loses heart; he cries or, in extreme cases, commits suicide. But as his inner knowledge and will power increase, he does not let himself be affected by the outer world and by what other people say or do. He becomes firm, like a rock.

"Develop equanimity. *[I was wondering how I could apply this to my life? I get moved and upset over things that are important for me, but perhaps not important for others. Today, for instance, I asked Ravindra to come for Swamiji's darshan, and he refused. I felt badly, why? Now, when I am convinced of the right action I will try not to be affected by what he or others say or do. I will just ignore their comments and try to remain calm and balanced.]*

"Give all your love to one person and see the results. *[But who is the person? I don't see anyone worthy, to whom I would give my love, fully. I would rather give it, or at least try to give it to God, a sadguru, or Swamiji, even though God or the idea of guru is still vague in my mind. But it is better to give love to God, or all that represents Him. Perhaps that's the inner meaning of what Swamiji is saying. Love should be given to all persons since God is in all.]*

"To be selfish is to be unethical, so be unselfish. Don't complain and think about yourself. Bear your sorrows or sufferings quietly. Don't go on telling others.

"No problem is great or small. Every problem is basic for the time when it lasts. There have to be problems, storms in life. Absolute silence and peace is only in the grave, so face them with equanimity. A migraine headache may seem worse to the person suffering it than another person's cancer. [*A person always feels his problem is worse or greater than another person's problem.*]

"Therefore, it is the mental attitude towards the problem that is important. No problem is so great that it should make you despair. As you grow spiritually, bigger problems also seem easy to resolve.

"You feel that you don't deserve all that is given to you, by His Grace. When a blessing is offered, take the opportunity, grasp it. If temptation comes, just say "go away."

"Have patience, work your way towards the Ultimate Reality. In time, you will realize it. [*Bless you Swamiji for these wonderful words*]. You cannot have the whole vision just at the beginning. When you go on a pilgrimage or to some new place, then you don't have the experience of what is there, but your knowledge about that place inspires you and creates the enthusiasm to go ahead. In the same way on the spiritual path, your knowledge gained through direct methods (reading books on the subject, and satsang) should, and will, make you feel enthusiastic and will spur you to continue on this path. Religion should be the way of life.

"A person due to his experiences in the world, of being rejected or made fun of, becomes inhibited and carries the experience in his future behavior. He does not feel confident about himself. Gradually, when he develops self-confidence he can face any person or circumstance and not feel afraid or inhibited. Such a person goes on in life with optimism, confidence, and enthusiasm."

"Swamiji," I asked, "What in short, is most important in *dharma* (essential truth, practiced as duty)?"

"Never hurt anyone consciously," Swamiji replied, "If you cannot spread happiness, at least do not add to the sorrow of this world."

I was so grateful for the opportunity to speak with Swamiji alone, and for forty-five minutes! To my surprise, he invited me to join him for breakfast. I just could not imagine how I was so lucky or worthy to have this wonderful opportunity.

While having breakfast, Swamiji chatted about himself and of his education at Lucknow University. Since I am from Lucknow, I thought he was joking but it actually was true. He then permitted me to have a photograph taken of the two of us together!

The following day I met Swamiji again. This time my husband Ravindra accompanied me. We spoke about faith in God and what was being done in the Chinmaya Mission centers all over India and in Sandeepany Sadhanalaya, the Vedanta University Swamiji founded in Bombay. This is where Swamiji would hold discourses and also teach students the principles of Vedanta when he was not traveling.

January 7, 1973
Sandeepany Sadhanalaya Ashram
Powai, Bombay

The Sandeepany Sadhanalaya, Swamiji's spiritual center, was built on a small hill near the Powai Lake, in the suburbs of Bombay. A huge *shivalinga*, the symbol of Lord Shiva as God in the aspect of the destroyer, adorns the peak of the temple. As I entered the temple I could see the form of Lord Shiva in marble, sitting in the *padmasana* (lotus) pose, smiling benevolently. There was also a shivalinga placed in the front of the temple for *puja* (prayer). Later on, the idol of Sri Krishna playing the flute and three silver urns filled with Ganga jal (water from the sacred river Ganga) were added on either side of Lord Shiva's statue.

To the right of the Sadhanalaya was a simple two-room *kutiya* (cottage) with a bathroom and a verandah. This is where Swamiji stayed. Since then, the verandah has been converted into a satsang hall where Swamiji would meet visitors. A statue of Swamiji's Guru, Pujya Tapovanji Maharaj, was placed nearby in the garden under a tree. Following Swamiji's mahasamadhi, a statue of Swamiji was placed in front of the kutiya. However, those who have seen Swamiji in person feel that no statue could accurately portray the expression and beauty of his radiant, serious yet compassionate eyes.

On the grounds of the Center there was also a *brahmacharin* (women's) hostel and a *brahmachari* (men's) hostel. These men and women were celibate students dedicated to spiritual growth. A library, dining hall, lecture hall and kutiyas for teachers completed the campus. In the coming years Swamiji would build a circular office wing and additional guest rooms with an open-air theater above the complex. The inauguration of the new wing took place in December 1991 on the eve of his *Tulabharam,* a ceremony in which he was weighed in gold on his seventy-fifth birthday.

During my frequent visits to Powai I would just soak in the peaceful atmosphere. The sounds of the birds chirping, the butterflies flitting among the fragrant flowers and the lush verdant foliage immediately brought on a feeling of deep calm. The powerful vedic chanting from the temple was mesmerizing. It was like an oasis in the desert of the concrete and steel city of Bombay. From the terrace near the temple I could view the glory of both sunrise and sunset. At night I could gaze at the moon and star filled skies. I was inspired to see and revere the living beauty of nature after a dark night or a long, hot afternoon. I could go on and on!

This was my first visit to the *Ashram* (residence and teaching center). Somehow Swamiji sensed my discomfort with being there. Addressing me he said, "If your husband doesn't like your being here, don't worry. Most of the time that is how it is." He continued, "Don't bother about other people, but if Ravindra doesn't want you to do something, don't do it. You should have harmony with one person, perfect harmony and understanding. Love him, and care for him." [*Honor your commitment to that one person.*]

Suddenly it became perfectly clear, even if I feel badly at times I should try not to hurt my husband. I should do what he wishes me to do, while remaining on my spiritual path. I thought, surely God will show me the way and give me the strength to walk steadily on.

Swamiji also addressed my concerns about the frequent house guests who stayed with us for lengthy periods of time. He instructed me to take care of their needs while setting aside a portion of my time for reading and meditation. "Things will somehow settle down," he told me. "Try to keep tranquil at all times."

He added, "You should not plan or even think of making a foreign visit when the children are there (home) and when they have school. In the case of a week or ten day business trip, you can plan to accompany him only if your mother is free to come to Bombay and look after the children. There is nothing like 'waiting silently', this is the highest meditation! In the second week of January, I can promise that if you come to visit us sometime, you shall find the place emblazoned with light and color, with sound and music. Lakshmi and Saraswati hand-in-hand, dancing on every stone, leaf, and flower, on the hills, down the slope, rolling from green turf to green turf. Do you know why? That guy called Chinmayananda will be there at the feet of Jagadeeswara. If you were to promise that every Tuesday you will be able to go to Powai any time during the day, and visit Jagadeeswara, he shall certainly start smiling as before."

On the same day, a friend from Calcutta accompanied me to Swamiji's ashram to attend his discourse on Adi Shankaracharya's *Vivekachoodamani*. This text explains how from Om, the state of Pure Consciousness, everything proceeds. When it is expressed through the body, mind and intellect equipment, pure consciousness identifies with the role it plays. Thus it creates the ego, the individual personality.

We are who we are because of the caliber of our mental and intellectual equipment. The texture and quality of this equipment depends upon innate tendencies, which are called *vasanas*. These tendencies and attitude carry themselves from one lifetime into the next. They are the unconscious, un-manifest imprints within us. The subtle impressions in the mind acquired from our past lives determine our future experiences and the field of their activity. Vasanas express themselves through our Body, Mind and Intellect. The individual becomes the Perceiver, Feeler and Thinker or the ego. When vasanas come into contact with Objects, Emotions and Thoughts, they manifest as actions.

Swamiji has explained it very clearly: "Vasanas veil the divinity in us and therefore they are known as ignorance.

However, due to our vasanas and consequent agitations of the mind, we become ignorant of our true nature and identify ourselves with our personality and its limitations."[1]

The following chart was used by Swamiji to explain the fundamentals of Vedanta. Pure Consciousness, denoted by the sound symbol Om, manifests in the world and expresses according to each person's own vasanas.

O M

V

B M I

P F T

O E T

Sound symbol (OM)
Indicates the higher reality

According to one's own
Vasanas (V)
Through the Body (B)
Mind (M)
Intellect (I)
The Perceiver (P), Feeler (F), Thinker (T)

Becomes enmeshed in the world of
Objects (O)
Emotions (E)
Thoughts (T)

Swamiji explaining the chart remarked, "You, the person, are the expression of your vasanas which are also called *samskaras*. Vasana, when expressing at the intellectual level manifests as desire, at the mental level as an agitation, and at the physical level as action.

"Desire should be controlled by *viveka*, discrimination, at the intellectual level. Agitation should be controlled by quieting the mind, as in surrender and meditation. Action should be controlled by dedicating all our work to God, as in *seva* or selfless activity.

"The following steps clearly explain this. First a desire manifests as a thought. Then that thought becomes an agitation at the emotional level. This agitation, so to speak, expresses as action at the body level. The result is either the fulfillment of desire which makes us happy and satisfies the ego, or an unfulfilled desire, which creates frustration, depression, or anger. This furthers the cycle of action and reaction.

"Our intellect determines the values in our life; namely, what is good and what is not good for us. We desire that which we consider good. Therefore, the spiritual seeker should cultivate positive values. Desire should be controlled not by suppression but by sublimation. This can be done through discernment and understanding at the intellectual level.

"All intelligent ways of exhausting old vasanas and not creating new ones are called yoga. All techniques done by a spiritual aspirant for enlightenment fall under the category of yoga. The path of action in the form of selfless service is called *karma* yoga. The path of love directed towards God in devotion is *bhakti* yoga, and with the intellect in the form of knowledge is *gyana* yoga."

Swamiji did not speak about *hatha* yoga, physical postures or asana, as this was not his path.

I am reminded of a discourse Swamiji gave in Lucknow in 1987, when he so beautifully elaborated on chapter VI, verse 24 of the Bhagavad Geeta about how you cannot know your own deep vasanas. They just express as your natural actions. All desires that do not originate from your own innate tendencies but are acquired either by hankering after what another individual possesses, or your own mental projections, in this context are called *sankalpas*. These types of desires, a *sadhaka* or seeker should give up.

A mahatma can know your samskaras, or deep-rooted inclinations, just by looking at you. Swami Akhandanandji immediately remarked when I first met him in Bombay in 1975, "*Tumhe satsang ka samskara hai*" (you have samskara for satsang).

January 15, 1973, Powai, Bombay

My understanding of Vedanta deepened during my conversations with Swamiji. I said, "It is amazing to hear about the Self, it seems as if a whole new vista has opened up." He replied, "My dear, just now what you see is one square inch from the total wall space, which is covered with the design and color of the whole tapestry, woven as the universe. Gradually when one sees the total design unveiled, then one can understand the beauty of harmony and balance, which is expressed throughout nature."

"Just now it is like hearing one line of Beethoven's masterpiece. When you hear the total symphony and its rhythm, the impact of the music is realized in the background of the silence within the heart. One gets absorbed and loses oneself in the music and the silence, created by the master musician, God!"

Swamiji was going for bhiksha to Kamala Krishnan's house that afternoon. Kamala Chanrai and I were accompanying him. While driving we noticed some animals on the street. Our talk turned towards the seven planes of consciousness and the fourteen *lokas* or worlds. Vedanta refers to the latter as fields of experience. Swamiji then spoke of rebirth, "Sometimes humans take birth in lower animal forms in order to quickly exhaust their animal vasanas. In these lower *yonis* (wombs) they do not accumulate new sins, only exhaust earlier ones."

The Geeta chanting prior to bhiksha was impressive. Hearing those divine sounds while being in Swamiji's holy presence brought tears to my eyes. This was my first bhiksha with Swamiji and we ate traditional South Indian food. Later Swamiji told me, "Tears inspired through devotion purify the heart."

January 26, 1973

Ravindra and I went to Powai for the morning discourse. Swamiji explained the concept of time. In the beginning there was One Reality or Consciousness. That first thought became aware of itself and from that first thought, another thought followed. In the space between the first and the second thought the concept of time arose. Thus the concept of 'space' and 'time' arise together in the mind.

While in Powai my husband and I extended an invitation to Swamiji to join us in Ahmedabad for the *khat muhurat*, ground breaking ceremony of our new house, to be held on February 5, 1973. Swamiji graciously accepted. It was on the same day that he was to lay the foundation stone for the construction of the Chinmaya Ashram in Ahmedabad.

Swamiji dressed in his temple clothes visits Neeranjali Hall, Trichur, 1976

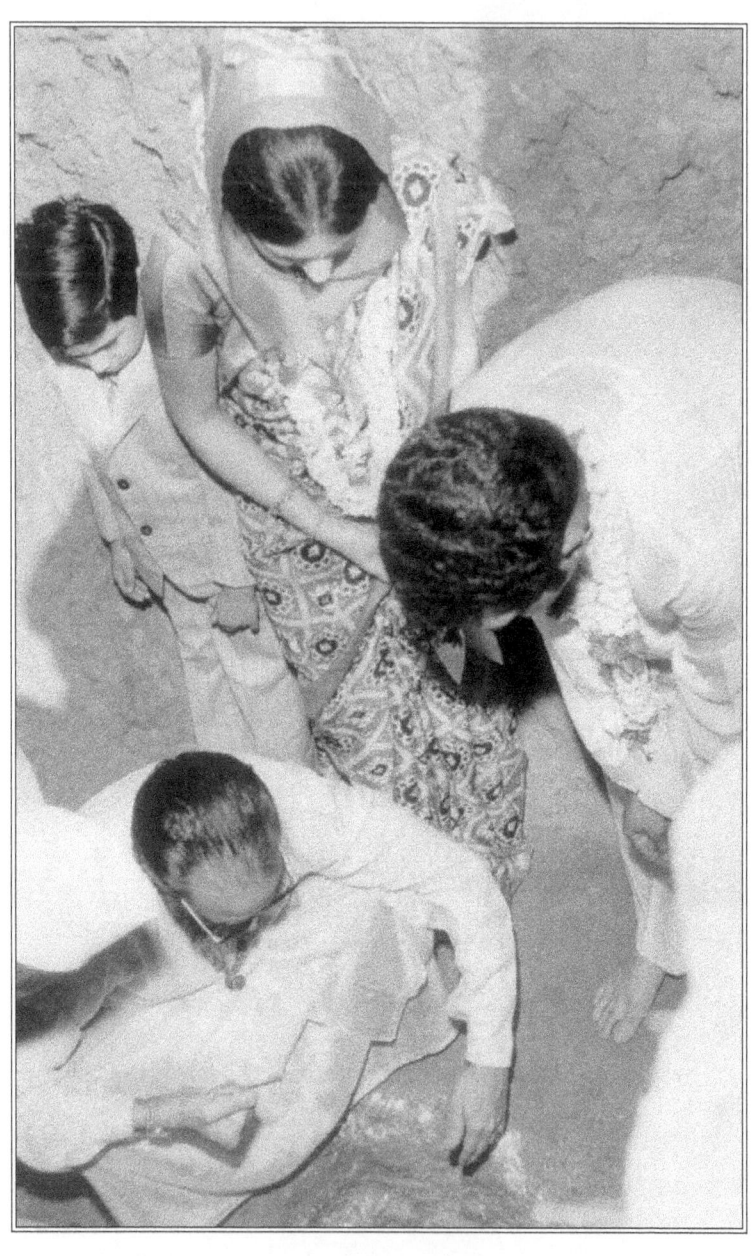

Swamiji laying the foundation stone for our house. My son Ashish is in the picture with Ravindra. Khat Mahurat, 5 February, 1973

February 5, 1973

*T*his was a most memorable and auspicious day for Ravindra and myself. A tent was set up at the site on which our home 'Ashreya' was to be built. There were about eighty people present. Most of our family members and close friends attended.

In the morning the president of Chinmaya Mission, Mrinaliniben Sarabhai, and the secretary, Shakuntalaben Desai, came with me to receive Swamiji at the airport. Kamala Chanrai accompanied him. We then proceeded directly to the foundation laying ceremony for the Mission.

At about ten o'clock, Swamiji came directly from the ceremony to the site of our new home. He sat smiling, quiet and serene, on a special seat that had been specially prepared for him. As is customary during a traditional ritual in India, the men and women sat separately on either side of Swamiji. After *pranams* (bowing down in reverence), we performed the "*Ganapathi Puja*" a prayer to God as the remover of obstacles, along with other rituals.

Swamiji laid the first foundation stone. He applied the cement on the brick with a silver spade, which we then kept as his *prasad* (blessing). Then Ravindra and I performed the brick laying ceremony. Water was poured while we chanted vedic mantras. During the ceremony Swamiji narrated a story to all the children who were there. After that, saffron and almond flavored milk was served to everyone.

Regarding our new house, Swamiji said, "I want the whole house, not just one room," and so it came to be; his presence is everywhere in the house and in all our hearts.

After the ceremony during an informal gathering, a few questions were presented to Swamiji. Ravindra's elder brother Rohitbhai asked, "Why misery?"

Swamiji answered, "We submit our own blueprint to be executed in this life. Later on our needs increase or change, thus the unfulfilled new desires create feelings of misery in the mind."

Navnitbhai, Ravindra's brother-in-law asked, "Will a house become a source of attachment?"

Swamiji answered, "Take it as His, the Lord's house, with you acting as the caretaker and thus living in it. Dedicate all actions to Him."

At noon we all went to Ravindra's ancestral home 'Ram Niwas'. Swamiji had bhiksha in the courtyard while sitting on a traditional Indian seat called *patla bajat*. Later in the day he went to Mrinaliniben Sarabhai's house for a visit. That same evening at the inauguration of Shakuntala Desai's painting exhibit, Swamiji spoke eloquently on art, inner beauty and harmony explaining how art expresses the beauty of the divine, quietens the mind and helps it strive towards excellence.

Ravindra and our children went back to Bombay. I accompanied them to the airport and then returned to Mrinaliniben's house where Swamiji was staying. It was nine o'clock in the evening and Swamiji had already retired to his room. He called me to join him. I didn't know it at the time, but it was on that day that my spiritual initiation was confirmed.

Swamiji returned my notebook in which I had expressed my thoughts and prayers to him. Inside he had written a beautiful page of acceptance. I didn't know the full depth of its meaning, but felt blessed that he had accepted me.

Swamiji's wrote, "As I have accepted you, your doubts etc. are my responsibility. I love you as you love me - this is what a guru does to a disciple. The action and reaction are equal - but not opposite. The only trouble with me is I am without time. All the hours are in the seva of all devotees. They multiply - but you are a special one. I don't know why."

As I talked to Swamiji all my thoughts and feelings came pouring out. I spoke about my fear that death is always shadowing us and life itself is short. The thought that five years earlier my father had suddenly passed away from a heart attack still haunted me. Now that I had Swamiji to guide me I didn't want to waste even one moment. But what could I do? "Swamiji, my relatives and my husband are not religious at all. They are all against this." I had tears in my eyes. Swamiji looked towards me with such compassion and affection. No

Neeru.

Ahmedabad
5.2.1973

As I have accepted you, your doubts etc are my responsibility. I love you as you love me —— this is what a Guru does to a disciple. The acharya & reacher are equal —— but not opposite.

The only trouble with me is I am with all time all the time. I have so many & all devotees. They multiply —— but you are a special one. I don't know why.

Sd/-

words could possibly describe such a look. Sitting across the table from me he said, "I will divert the course of this current situation against you. Don't worry, together we will spread the message of true dharma throughout the world."

I prostrated and Swamiji stood up. He helped me get up and embraced me. A current of energy passed through me. As I stood at the door I asked him to take me to Uttarkashi. I stupidly blurted that someone had told Ravindra and me that our previous birth had been there. He just smiled while remaining silent. His eyes were moist and full of kindness and love. Oh, how I wish I could keep that picture in my mind always. I was fortunate to have him look at me with such compassion on several other occasions. Once in April 1973, while we were in the plane flying from Bombay to Lucknow, and again during a satsang in Lucknow.

My feelings at that time are best described by verse 35 from Adi Shankara's text *Vivekachoodamani*:

Svaamin namaste, nata lokbandho
Karunya sindho patitam bhavabhdau
Mamudharatmiya katakshadrishtaya
Rijvyat karunyasudhabhivrishtayaa

O Master, O friend of those who reverentially surrender to thee, thou ocean of mercy, I salute thee; save me, fallen as I am into this sea of worldly existence, with a direct glance from thy eyes, which rains nectarine grace supreme

It was on this heavenly night that I had a mystical dream-like vision of Swamiji saving my life. Vivid scenes of caves, orange-robed *sanyasis* (monks), rituals, *murtis* (idols) and me, lying dead. Swamiji was blowing life-giving breath into my mouth, reviving me. I wondered about the deep impact this vision would have on me. Afterwards, I understood. It was a confirmation of my initiation and acceptance by Swamiji, who humbled my ego, bringing to life a new person.

Ten years later I went to Swamiji's ashram in Sidhabari in the Dhauladhar mountain range of the Himalayas. Just as in my dream I saw orange-robed sanyasis and brahmacharis who were living in small cave-like dwellings. It was at this ashram that I had strong spiritual experiences with Swamiji, especially during my stay in November 1991 when Swamiji was recuperating from illness. I was once again reminded of this dreamlike vision.

Kumbhabhishekham at Powai Temple, Bombay, December 1974

Neeru with Swamiji after Shivaratri puja in Powai Ashram.

FEBRUARY, 1973
POWAI, BOMBAY

*O*NE MORNING, when I went to meet Swamiji at his ashram, I found some devotees sitting on the doorsteps of Swamiji's kutiya. They told me, "You cannot go in." I waited outside for quite some time.

Later when I met Swamiji, he asked me "Where were you till now? I was waiting for you." I told him what had happened. He said, "Listen, remember this, you come directly to the Swami, don't ask other devotees, and do not ever compare yourself with any other devotee. Everyone has their own place."

Since Ravindra was out of town, I had planned to spend the entire day at the ashram. I was dressed in a simple white printed sari manufactured by our own textile mill. Swamiji asked me to go with him to Jamnadas's house for *namkaran samskara* or naming ceremony of his son. Jamnadas was a trustee of Chinmaya Mission. I was thrilled to be asked and immediately said, "Yes. But won't my clothes look odd?"

He responded, "You are dressed for going out with the Swami." The lady who came to pick us up asked me who I was. I was wondering what to say, but before I could answer Swamiji spoke, "Say you are the Swami's shishya." After the naming ceremony, Swamiji played lovingly with

Jamanadas's son. He gave him his own *mala* (traditional prayer beads) and named him Janardana which means one who serves the people.

During the drive back to the ashram, the topic of my having a child arose. Swamiji joked, "How about the Canadian?" We had earlier mentioned to Swamiji, Ravindra's desire to have another child. At that time he had told me "you need not have any more." I told Swamiji about Ravindra's desire to have the child born in Canada or the United States. He said, "You should not say no. If it is in your *prarabdha* or destiny, better to have it now rather than take another birth."

Swamiji was sitting on the terrace one evening along with some devotees. When I arrived Swamiji referred to me, "She is the last but not the least." He continued, "One gets, according to the strength one has of receiving." Regarding my question as to whether or not there has been progress in my achieving *gyana* or spiritual knowledge, he said to me, "Another ten years."

On another occasion Swamiji said to me "It is not easy to become one of my close ones." He invited me to come to his room while he was having bhiksha. Swamiji said, "Very intimate ones are allowed in the bedroom while Swami has food."

Two sisters, devotees of Swamiji, brought Swamiji his meal. Later he gave me some prasad to eat saying, "Through penance, what I have cooked up I am giving. Eat, you have to just eat and digest." He was referring to the knowledge he had gained through intense austerities and which he was now giving us while we remained in the comfort of our homes.

FEBRUARY 24, 1973
POWAI, BOMBAY

THE RENOWNED SAINT Sri Ma Anandamayi (Ma signifies respected mother) visited the ashram. I was so excited about her visit that I brought a red carpet from home to be spread in front of the dais where Swamiji sat with his guest under a canopy of flowers. Seeing Ma and Swamiji together was an uplifting experience. In the temple, I glided into *dhyana* (contemplation). Tears just flowed. I was a silent witness. At Swamiji's request Ma sang a beautiful devotional song or bhajan and soon everyone present joined her in singing. Jagadeeswara's temple had turned into *Brahmaloka*, the highest level of heaven!

Swamiji and Ma were going to the house of a devotee in the suburb of Bandra and I was invited to go with them. Just as I was getting into the car I realized that in all of my excitement I had forgotten to wear my sandals. I went anyway, just the way I was, barefoot. The famous singers Sudha

Malhotra and Purushottam Jalota sang devotional songs. Ma and Baba, (Baba, signifies respected father) as Ma liked to call Swamiji, sat together. What a sight! I felt I had been transported to another realm, beyond time and space.

On the way back, Swamiji placed a garland made of dry fruits and cardamom around my neck. This had been given to him earlier by our host. He said sweetly, "You deserve it today." I was overwhelmed with joy.

FEBRUARY 1973
POWAI, BOMBAY

*A*FTER THE EVENING LECTURE, a group of people met with Swamiji and invited him to attend the centenary celebration of a great soul Swami Ram Tirtha. In their introduction of Swami Chinmayananda they referred to him as a *siddha-purusha* or realized person. Swamiji extolled Swami Ram Tirtha as a great Vedantin master for whom he had the highest regard. In fact, I was instructed to read his complete works, *In the Woods of God Realization*.

Some of the other writings that Swamiji had asked me to read were *The Gospel of Sri Ramakrishna* and the *Complete Works* of Swami Vivekananda. Swamiji often referred to them as great masters.

There is a story about Ramakrishna Paramhansa which shows how his sense of identification and oneness with God manifested even on his body. The story goes that he was sitting on his verandah watching a cow graze in front of his cottage. A brahmachari tried to drive away the cow but with no success. He then hit the cow several times with a stick and suddenly heard Sri Ramakrishna cry out in pain. To the horror of the brahmachari, there were red welts on Sri Ramakrishna's back. These welts showed the extent of which he could feel the soul of the animal as his own.

Every day I would take notes on whatever topic Swamiji had addressed during satsang and then give them to him to read over. He would keep them for a few days and then return them to me with his comments.

FEBRUARY 26, 1973
WORLI SEA FACE, BOMBAY

SWAMIJI GRACED OUR HOUSE for an informal bhiksha. Only my family members were present. I was nervous as well as excited. While he was there we did a puja which involved a ritual of performing an *aarti*. Aarti is an offering of a lit flame to a master or an idol of a deity. *Aa* means 'towards' and *rati* means 'the highest love for God.' During the aarti the wick would not stay lit. Swamiji taught us how to take the cotton wool and make a rounder wick at the base, twist the other end into a point and dip it into *ghee* (clarified butter). Once we followed these instructions the *diya* (small lamp) always burnt steadily. Swamiji told us, "Always light a lamp before performing any puja or auspicious ceremony."

The reason for Swamiji taking such interest in teaching us how to make a lamp burn correctly became clear to me at a later time. The sadguru unveils the light of consciousness within. The seeker must be aware of this before starting any auspicious work. The mind will behave correctly according to this light of discrimination. In order to keep the flame burning steadily, the tip of the wick, which represents our heart, should be made single-pointed towards the goal. The base of the wick, which represents our mind, should be solid and firm like the knowledge of the true Self. The oil or ghee in which we dip our mind is the love towards the goal. Such a lamp, like our personality, will burn steadily and spread its light around for everyone.

Swamiji told me "You are a *kora kagaz* (blank paper). I can write easily on you." I did not know anything about Hindu rituals at that time, so I did whatever he told me to do. I had no preconceived ideas of my own. I didn't even know how one was to interact with a guru and my behavior was very spontaneous. Swamiji even wrote out my

Chinmaya Mission membership application and as a way of introduction, He wrote "Chinmaya devotee." He advised me to remember that the spiritual path has to be walked alone and not just by becoming a mission member. He said, "It is easier for a teacher to write on a blank paper of the devotee's heart than to have to first remove the blotches of preconceived erroneous notions that only fatten the ego."

March 1, 1973
Bombay

The evening before the *Shivaratri* festival, Swamiji asked us to take him into town. Since another Swami was already sitting in the front seat of the car, Swamiji had to sit in the back with Indira Rohira and myself. This was unusual for him as he always sat in the front.

On the return drive, we talked about how one's personality is reflected by their style of dress. I asked Swamiji, "How about me?" He replied, "You dress all right. Girls from cultured families needn't be told how to dress. Some women really dress in a vulgar and cheap way; long nails, see through *saris*, no *bindi*." He went on, "My Ma Anandamayi is the most beautiful lady in the world, be like her. Her face reflects *sattwa* (purity). It is serene and smiling, totally without vasanas." In December 1974 while visiting Ma Anandamayi in her ashram in the sacred pilgrimage town of Naimisharanya, I told Ma what Swamiji had said about her.

We also spoke about the story of Eklavya (from the ancient Hindu epic, Mahabharata). This devoted disciple cut his thumb off and gave it to his guru as *gurudakshina* (offering to the teacher). I said to Swamiji, "When the guru, or God, knows that his own devotee is able to bear the separation between himself and his beloved guru, then and only then will he allow the devotee to stay away." Swamiji laughed and said, "You are smart. You have it all in you," He paused for a few moments then went on, "but you don't have *vairagya* (detachment). There are still desires, vasanas, which are in the subconscious mind and you are not even aware of them. It is because of them that you have taken up this body and they have to be fulfilled and exhausted."

MARCH 2, 1973
POWAI, BOMBAY

*I*T WAS SHIVARATRI, a day dedicated to worshipping Lord Shiva. It was also the anniversary of the day Swamiji took *sanyasa* (vows of renunciation). I fasted in honor of Lord Shiva and my Guru. Swamiji came out of his seclusion only once during that day. To me he looked like Lord Shiva Himself, with wet unruly locks of hair, eyes half closed in a silent meditative mood. He had come to the temple for Lord Shiva's aarti. There was a group of devotees chanting "*Om Namah Shivaya*" (prostrations to Lord Shiva), which is chanted continuously for twenty-four hours on this auspicious day.

MARCH 11, 1973
DELHI

I TRAVELED WITH SWAMIJI to Uttarkashi in North India. Our first stop was Delhi where we were joined by Indira Rohira and Asha Chanrai. We stayed at Jagdeesh Prasad's house. He was a Trustee of the Chinmaya Mission. The millions of doubts that I had earlier started subsiding. I was so calm and happy, just like a child while in Swamiji's presence. As I made his bed and brought water to his room, Swamiji commented, "Ravindra should see you working now."

March 13, 1973

Swamiji looked after me as a father would care for his child. On the morning of March 13th we left for Haridwar en route to Rishikesh and Uttarkashi. Indira, Asha and I were in Swamiji's car and my uncle and aunt followed us in theirs. On the way we sang *guru stotra* which is a hymn dedicated to the teacher and many other bhajans. The drive was so enjoyable that it seemed as if we reached our destination in no time at all. The Sadhu Bela Ashram, situated on the banks of the sacred river Ganga, was a tranquil place. We got out of the car and proceeded directly to the river. It was my first holy dip and I was blessed to have Swamiji direct me into the Ganga water. We all took three dips, which signify the purification of the three bodies: the gross body, subtle body and causal body.

In Haridwar we had lunch and rested for a while. Swamiji seemed a little tired. His pulse was irregular so we decided to get a doctor to check his heart. Swamiji joked and said, "My heart misses beats because according to the law of *karma* (cause and effect) millions of lives were left still to be lived but God, in His Grace, wanted to liberate this soul in this very life time. In order to fulfill the destiny of those lives, He kills me every three or four beats. My heart stops and then starts again; a new birth."

What a way to glorify the Lord! Even while he was in physical pain he kept smiling in order to teach us equanimity.

In the evening Swamiji gave a talk on the 'Secret of Action' at the auditorium of Bharat Heavy Engineering company. Later, during bhiksha Swamiji referring to my cooking said, "You are useless, you don't know anything. Otherwise I would take you to USA." I replied, "I'll learn South Indian cooking. I'll do anything for you."

"Anything?" He asked. "Yes," I answered.

On our final day in Haridwar, while talking to my aunt and uncle on the banks of the Ganga, Swamiji referred to me, saying, "She is like a stone." I reflected on the meaning of this. Immovable as a stone, or was I like the stone that could be shaped into any form the sculptor wished?

The following day we left for the ashram in Uttarkashi. This is where Swamiji had studied at the feet of his guru, revered Swami Tapovanji Maharaj. Swamiji was in a relaxed and happy mood as he listened to us singing bhajans. He reminisced about his college years and said, "I feel like sitting near you and talking about my motor bike days and my student life at Butler Hostel in Lucknow University." He recalled the time he mistakenly told his servant to bring him water in a *razai* (quilt) instead of a *surai* (earthen ware jug) because he was not fluent in Hindi! These little anecdotes of Swamiji revealed his human side. He used his subtle sense of humor to teach us how not to take life so seriously.

March, 1973
Uttarkashi

*U*ttarkashi brought out the light-hearted spirit in Swamiji, "I feel young again, as if I have come back home," he said. The ashram was serene and quiet. The first sound we heard was the river *Ma Ganga* humming *Oham Om*, the sound of creation. There was a faint sound of tinkling bells as the breeze gently played with them. I immediately felt a deep spiritual peace within. We offered pranams at the hut of our grand guru, Swami Tapovanji Maharaj.

The beauty of this magnificent place, nestled among the majestic Himalayan mountains, which support the banks of the holy river Ganga, is truly beyond words. But I will do my best to give you a glimpse of its splendor.

On the banks of the Ganga, near the Uttarkashi ashram, are simple kutiyas. These belong to other small ashrams which are scattered on different levels of the mountain. The sound of the heavenly flow of the Ganga, and the powerful strength of the Himalayas, create an atmosphere that is totally unique. One cannot help but be cleansed in both body and soul after living in such a sacred spot. The silent prayers and meditations of pious souls, visible mahatmas, as well as those in the astral plane, add to the purifying and elevating vibrations of the location.

Swamiji had intentionally assigned a particular devotee to share my room because he wanted me to understand how the grace and protection of a master works. My roommate shared her story with me. One night while in Uttarkashi, she was feeling devastated because that day her divorce had been finalized. Her marital problems had created much upheaval in her family. During satsang that night she did not say a word to Swamiji but she felt like ending it all by jumping into the river Ganga. Exactly at the moment that very thought entered her mind, Swamiji took off his watch and tied it to her wrist. Gradually her mind calmed down and she regained her balance. Later on Swamiji helped her family reaffirm their unity and affection for each other.

It was a treat to watch Shivaraman, Swamiji's attendant of many years, making tea for Swamiji in the pre-dawn hours. He would pour the steaming tea from one glass into another, keeping quite a distance between the two, thereby creating lots of foam on top of the tea. This is a typical Indian way of cooling tea.

Indira would help in the kitchen with the cooking where a log fire would be burning in the old style *chulhas* (clay stoves). We would sit down on the floor in a nearby room and enjoy simple yet delicious *sattwic* (pure) food. Since then an extension has been built with more modern facilities in the kitchen as well as other areas. Swami

Tapovan Maharaj's small mud-floor hut has been kept as it was during his lifetime with its sacred atmosphere intact.

The terrace in front of Swamiji's kutiya was glistening as if a silver sheet had been laid down as a welcoming mat. There were no sounds to be heard other than the soft murmur of the flowing Ganga. The atmosphere felt charged with a powerful energy. It was as if time had stopped still. The absence of sound spoke more than the presence of a thousand words.

The essence of truth is always conveyed in silence. Swamiji never performed any specific ritual or ceremony while bestowing grace on the disciple. This grace was always given whenever the disciple's ego was absent and he or she was lovingly attentive and least expecting such an honor.

We sat quietly for a moment. Swamiji then lifted his right foot and with his toe gently outlined a circle in the region of my heart. I felt Swamiji showering me with his love, purifying me, both body and soul. I was transformed, in a dreamlike state of ecstasy, at the feet of such an exalted master! There was only ONE presence. One, without form and without thought.

Swamiji's slow serious voice brought me back to earth. He first spoke in Hindi, "*Yeh mano laya hai, par mera mano naasha ho gaya hai.* This is *laya*, the temporary absorption of the mind. However, I have destroyed my ego mind."

In *mano laya* the mind temporarily gets absorbed into a higher spiritual state but the ego remains. Whereas *mano naasha* signifies the complete anhilation of the ego mind once and for all. This theme has been extensively commented upon by Sri Ramana Maharshi, a famous spiritual master of the twentieth century. In the book *Talks with Ramana Maharshi*[1], he takes it a step further saying, "*Mano-nasha, jyana* and *chittaikagrata* (annihilation of the mind, knowledge and one-pointedness) means the same."

In a flash it finally struck me that Swamiji is a master who has transcended his ego mind.

Never wanting to waste a moment away from Swamiji, I'd wake up early in the morning. At 4 a.m. I would take a bath in icy cold water and spend nearly the entire day in Swamiji's presence, sitting in his study which faced the terrace and the river Ganga beyond. The sound of Om surrounded me.

I was in a pensive mood one day, as I sat sorting Swamiji's mail. Swamiji noticed this and said, "How did you become a mother of two? Smile always and never cry. I don't like tears. Vedantins are one in Him." With Swamiji I experienced oneness. We are physically two, yet one in essence!

Swamiji took us to the temple of Lord Vishwanath in Uttarkashi. He asked the temple priest to chant vedic mantras and to guide me as I performed *abhishek* (ritual of bathing an idol) of Lord Vishwanath with milk and holy Ganga water. The three days that we spent in Uttarkashi were truly blessed and beyond earthly description.

March, 1973
Bombay

*M*y sister Preeta, who lives in USA, visited Bombay. She had found out about my new spiritual interests and was very concerned for me. "What is this I've been hearing about you following a Swami and becoming deeply involved in mystic life?" Wanting so much to share my new joy and excitement and end her worries about me, I asked Preeta to meet Swamiji for herself. She agreed and together we went to Powai.

Swamiji was sitting on the terrace in front of the temple. During the evening aarti, vedic chants were being recited. Preeta was so moved by Swamiji's presence that she went up to him, and with tears running down her cheeks, she knelt down and bowed at his feet. She later told me that she had felt like Mary Magdalene surrendering at the feet of her Master, Jesus Christ, with his compassion purifying and consoling her heart. Swamiji's love encompasses even those who are not spiritual practitioners. In time Preeta came to serve Swamiji with great love.

APRIL, 1973
PILANI, RAJASTHAN

*O*N THE FIFTH OF APRIL, Preeta and I left for Pilani to be with Swamiji. After three long weeks of being separated from him my prayers were being answered. We would have three days together; just Swamiji, Preeta and myself.

This was Swamiji's first visit to Pilani. In the mornings there were talks on the "Logic of Spirituality" and in the evenings the topic was "The Fundamentals of Vedanta." We stayed on the campus of the Birla Institute of Technology. Pilani is very hot, especially in April and the house was old without any air-conditioning. Swamiji very sweetly told us "I become the air, to embrace and surround you with my cooling effect," and really, we never felt the heat. The rooms were quite large with high ceilings and a beautiful verandah where Swamiji would have his tea and breakfast. One morning while he was sitting there watching the sunrise, Swamiji said, "Our Gurudev is giving darshan." He was referring to his guru Swami Tapovanji Maharaj who took his *vidwat sanyas* (renunciation by way of knowledge) with the sun as his witness. The sun shining in its majestic splendor reminded Swamiji of his guru.

Swamiji was very relaxed, enjoying this rare opportunity to be informal. He was smiling and joking, throwing bits of bread to the birds and the peacocks who pirouetted proudly.

One evening while the three of us were sitting in the drawing room Swamiji said, "Sometimes I feel I am just doing nothing." He may have said that just to see what our reaction would be. I answered, "You are doing the most noble task, giving true knowledge."

Swamiji, noticing that there was a wooden floor in the large room suddenly said, "It is ideal for dancing." I told him that I didn't know how to dance western style, so he promptly said he would teach me and proceeded to do just that. Swamiji went on to explain how he had learned to waltz during his days as a student in Lucknow, when he would go for dances at the famous Carlton Hotel.

Rarely have I seen Swamiji so at ease. "It is so nice to be able to sit informally, without being serious in a spiritual guru's role, just relaxed, no puja, just informal simple living," he told us. I now think this was Swamiji's way of seeing whether this informal behavior of his, brought any change in our attitude of reverence or *gurubhava* towards him. In fact, it increased our respect and devotion for him.

Our hosts sent Swamiji a car to use during his stay. We had already rented an air-conditioned car for him, but Swamiji told us to return it. Out of respect for our hosts, we would use the car they had offered him. Even though the car did not have air-conditioning and was much less comfortable, Swamiji was always in good cheer. By his actions he was teaching us to be tranquil and smile at all times, not to hurt anyone's feelings just to gain some material comfort.

During the drive back to Delhi we sang many bhajans. Swamiji sang "Hare Rama Hare Krishna," and then he chanted a Sanskrit *shloka* (verse) from *Mukundmala*. This text was written by a South Indian Malayalee King who was a devotee of Sri Krishna. Swamiji then translated this shloka into English for us:

Krsna tvadiya-pada-pankaja-panjarantah
Adyaiva me visatu manasa-raj-hamsah!
Prana-prayana-samaye-kapha-vata-pittaih
Kanthavarodhana-vidhau smaranam kutaste

Oh, Krishna may the royal swan of my mind enter today itself into the nest of your lotus feet.
How can one otherwise be sure of remembering you later, when one's *pranas* are leaving one's body
[one is in the throes of death], with phlegm, wind and bile, [blocking one's throat and making breathing itself difficult]

Here, the urgency to cultivate devotion for God is highlighted by the words *adya-iva*, which means 'now itself.'

April 14, 1973
Worli Sea Face, Bombay

After attending a Vishwa Hindu Parishad (World Hindu Organization) meeting at Mr. Kamdar's house, Swamiji came to my house and stayed the night. The following day he asked me to accompany him to Shantilal Somaiya's printing press. We were going to check the printing of the hardbound version of Swamiji's Holy Geeta commentary.

On the way home Shantilal Somaiya, his father and Ram Batra, a Trustee of the Central Chinmaya Mission Trust (C.C.M.T.) and Swamiji's close devotee, were in the car with us. Swamiji said, "One day she (Neeru) will rewrite the essence of Upanishads in such a way that even people in the west can read it, in a relaxed way, sitting near a swimming pool."

I couldn't believe what I had just heard. I thought he must be joking! I told Swamiji that I didn't think I would ever be able to write. Now I know better. So many words of Swamiji have come true.

Shantilal Somaiya told Swamiji, "Your disciple is not listening to your command."

I immediately retorted, "You are like *Narada* (a mythological figure, who would create conflict between a devotee and God, in order to inspire devotional thought) trying to create a rift between me and Swamiji."

Supporting me, Swamiji said, "She is under training and will have to visit USA with me to know the mood, the people, their ways."

Shantilalji then smiled at me.

APRIL 17, 1973
EN ROUTE FROM BOMBAY TO POONA

We left early in the morning for a day trip to Poona. Swamiji was to give a talk to the Girl Guides and Boy Scouts at the home of Mr Vissanji, a Trustee of the Mission. There were four of us in the car, Swamiji, Preeta, my sister-in-law Vinita and myself. During the drive Swamiji chanted shlokas from the Bhagavad Geeta, chapter II. It was a treat to hear Swamiji chant. I remember wishing that I had brought a tape recorder with us on the trip. Swamiji was in the mood to talk. He told Vinita, "Do not expect praise from others. Do your duty, otherwise it is like expecting a tip, as waiters do, for serving customers of the restaurant where they work."

I told Swamiji that I had finished reading *Atmabodha* and his book *Meditation and Life*. He just glared at me and said, "Finished? Never finished!" He also seemed annoyed with me when I mentioned Ramana Maharshi and *How to Meditate*. I quickly got the message. How could I talk of such greatness so casually. First I must learn to be quiet I thought. Throughout the journey I felt him snub me many times. I realized it must have been to annihilate the stupid ego that always wants to show off what it has learned.

There was very little talk during the drive back to Bombay. Swamiji used this time to read some of his mail. We reached Powai around 9 p.m. and discovered that due to a power failure there was no electricity. Then just as we entered the gates of the ashram our car had a flat tire. Thank goodness Swamiji didn't notice it at all.

Shivaraman, Swamiji's devoted attendant, was waiting for his return with a flashlight in hand.

After the long and tiring day Swamiji was relaxing in his office when I asked if we could sit with him for a while. He suddenly became angry and said that we should go home. I was so upset with myself. Why did I have to make Swamiji angry? I must not be worthy of being his disciple. We had the tire repaired and went home.

I spent that entire night sobbing silently; I was so remorseful. This must be what is called a sin.

Swamiji had explained that a sin is an angle of deviation between what we know to be correct and what we do which is contrary to it. In other words an error. Why can't I be quiet? How could I face him again? I thought of sending Swamiji a note, asking permission to see him. I was already regretting my behavior.

APRIL 18, 1973
BOMBAY

*A*SHA KAMDAR, KAMALA CHANRAI AND I had invited forty devotees to my house for bhiksha, expecting Swamiji to be there as well. I went to Powai with Preeta and straight to the temple to pray to Lord Jagadeeswara with Swamiji on my mind. Still upset with what had transpired yesterday I asked Preeta to go and see Swamiji, which she did. When Preeta returned to the temple she told me, "Swamiji is calling for you." Nervously, and feeling quite shattered, I went to see him.

As I entered the office in his cottage, Swamiji was smiling at me. It felt like the sun was shining, removing all the clouds from my heart, but still, I hesitated. He called my name "Nee...ru, Neeru." I was doing pranams when

Swamiji held my hands and looked into my eyes with the most kind and loving glance, I melted. Swamiji exclaimed, "You were thinking of writing a note to me? You think I don't know what is going on in your mind?" He continued, "I am so sorry for last night's outburst. I was tired and it was hot."

It was his love and compassion that made Swamiji sweetly apologize to me. As if he had to! I immediately responded, "Swamiji, I was upset with myself and felt unworthy of being your disciple. I caused you to become angry because of me." Looking into my sad eyes he said, "This is true love." These were soothing words for my repenting heart. "What if I don't come to your place for bhiksha?" He said this jokingly, knowing that I had already invited many devotees. I smiled and answered back, "So, what's that got to do with me? I'll remain here with you."

Initially the treatment given by the teacher may hurt, but in the long run it is healing. In his invisible way Swamiji teaches and cures the disease of the *samsari maya* (worldly illusion) of attachment.

Around noon I went back home with Preeta. I spent the afternoon preparing for the bhiksha and then rushed back to Powai to escort Swamiji to my house. It was a ninety minute drive but I never noticed the traffic or the distance.

May 6, 1973
National Geeta Gyana Yagna
Bangalore

*M*y husband, children and my youngest sister, Shubhra [now a spiritual teacher known as Shubhraji], accompanied me to Bangalore to attend the National Geeta Gyan Yagna. It was a ten day lecture series and Swamiji was to speak on the Bhagavad Geeta, chapter II in the evening. The morning text was *Purusha Suktam*, a vedantic hymn dedicated to the Creator. Purusha Suktam is one of the most famous hymns in the *Rig Veda*. It describes how the Infinite Reality expressing through its creativeness becomes God, the Creator or *Ishwara*. When Ishwara identifies with the urge to create, he himself expresses as the individualized ego or *jiva*.

This sublime hymn contains eighteen verses of praise adoring the mighty divine spirit which can be reached through yagna. Swamiji explained yagna as sacrifice in the spirit of co-operative endeavor for the welfare of the whole community, as Lord Krishna expounds in chapter III, verse X of the Geeta.

I find that the first verse of the Purusha Suktam draws me easily into a contemplative mood:

Sahasra seershaa Purushah
Sahasra akshah sahasra path
Sa bhoomin vishwatho vrittwa
Atya tishttat dashangulam

Purusha is the Supreme Consciousness. It is poetically depicted as a Cosmic Being with a thousand heads, eyes and legs. This Purusha envelops the entire earth as well as transcends it by the length of ten-fingers which implies all the ten directions. All that was, is, and will be, is nothing but this immortal Purusha.

Given the importance of the Purusha Suktam, Swamiji had instructed the initiates to memorize this text within four days. On the fifth day of the yagna, Swamiji asked all of the brahmacharis to recite it. Seeing that hardly any of them could do so, Swamiji, like the strict teacher he was, announced, "Today no lunch will be served to all the brahmacharis. They will fast. Tomorrow, in the morning class I expect all of you to recite the Purusha Suktam."

We all felt sorry for the brahmacharis, but deep within our hearts we knew that it was the sincere concern for our spiritual growth that prompted the Master to take such a measure.

Swamiji, as a teacher, maintained a disciplined atmosphere around him just by his mere presence. He never hesitated to convey his thoughts and managed this simply by a glance or a facial expression. Sometimes it was in the form of a bitter pill delivered with a sugar coated smile. At other times it was simply a loving look. It all depended upon the recipient's sincerity as a seeker.

    A spiritual master works in unique ways. Swamiji, though a strict disciplinarian, was also full of compassion. I was reminded of an incident that reveals this quality. A longtime devotee and initiate was found to be terminally ill. To speed up her spiritual evolution Swamiji decided to give her *sanyas diksha* (the final vows of renunciation) while she was in the hospital. He did this over the phone since he was traveling overseas. He told the devotees who were with him that this would accelerate her spiritual progress even before she left the earthly plane. Every action of his was for the greatest welfare of the seekers around him.

    Swamiji brushed aside convention and adopted his own unique approach to things. Once when I had my monthly period I asked another member of my family to take Swamiji his morning tea. He would usually have tea while going through his mail, which poured in from all over the world. When I met him later to offer pranams he asked me why I had sent the tea through someone else. I told him the reason. Swamiji smiled and quietly said, "Though the general rule is that ladies should wash their hair on the fourth day while bathing and only then attend to pujas or rituals it does not stop them from doing japa mentally."

Swamiji continued, "I have permitted you to do all my personal work or seva hence do not worry. You go ahead with the normal routine in my presence. For puja and rituals in the temple you may follow the traditional rules."

While in Bangalore we stayed at the Ashoka Hotel. I was privileged to be asked by Swamiji to be in his personal service; this is one of the ways that a master trains his student. At five o'clock in the morning I would bring him tea. I took care of Swamiji's clothes, cleaned his room and served him breakfast and dinner. Lunch was usually *samashti bhiksha*, a group meal. I brought Swamiji a glass of milk every night which he would graciously accept. It wasn't until much later that I learned he didn't like to drink milk at night. This opportunity to serve him helped to open my heart even more.

Sometimes Swamiji would remark, "You are useless, how did mummy get you?" Again, I thought, he is at the job of ego blasting. I asked him how I could remove my weaknesses and improve myself and he replied, "Remain as you are. Mona Lisa's smile is just right. Can any change be made?"

During the inauguration of the Bangalore lecture series, attended by thousands from all over India, we were fortunate enough to be sitting close to the stage. From this vantage point we had a clear view of the event presided over by His Holiness Sri Satya Sai Baba, another spiritual leader. Later when Swamiji spoke, it was as if Lord Krishna himself was present.

He told the audience how, from the time of Krishna's birth and throughout his life, Krishna demonstrated the skills of perfection by acting without attachment, inspiring others to do the same. His greatest gift to his beloved devotee and friend Arjuna was the message of surrender to the highest goal, the all-pervading, all-knowing Lord of the universe. This can be achieved through the art of living intelligently as written by Veda Vyasa in the Bhagavad Geeta. The Geeta addresses three paths for an individual seeking perfection; karma yoga or the path of action, bhakti yoga or the path of devotion and gyana yoga or the path of knowledge.

The Bhagavad Geeta was like the Holy Bible for the great Indian leader Mahatma Gandhi and other freedom fighters in India. They achieved independence for our nation from the British through the principles of non-violence and non-cooperation.

The evening discourse was on chapter II of the Bhagavad Geeta. This famous text is a dialogue between Lord Krishna and the confused prince Arjuna set against the backdrop of a battlefield. Arjuna is faced with an inevitable war of justice as his cousins refuse to return the kingdom which they had usurped. Even though Arjuna realizes that he needs to stand up against the forces of negativity, his own emotional involvement with his cousins clouds his intellect. Arjuna represents all spiritual seekers. Arjuna has problems which he cannot resolve due to a conflict over his personal values and the nature of action required of him. In this conflicted state Arjuna recognizes Krishna as a higher identity in whom he has faith and surrenders to him. He asks for Krishna's advice in order to decide the right course of action. Krishna, in the role of a friend and guru, is aware of Arjuna's dilemma and helps him to resolve his confusion.

Krishna explains to Arjuna that man cannot escape from the duties he has to perform in his life; towards himself, his family and society. These duties are based on the eternal values of life or dharma. The best course of action is to understand the truth through knowledge. One should not become sorrowful even when faced with an unpleasant task that one has to perform. Merely by listening to this discourse Arjuna is transformed and becomes ready to face the challenge.

The Bangalore yagna was a wonderful learning experience for me. Among other things, I noticed how petty jealousies exist even among spiritual seekers; something one might not expect to find. Truly speaking, treading on the path of spirituality can be fraught with many obstacles. I observed my own mind and learned to slowly navigate the world of relationships with mindfulness and sensitivity.

We left Bangalore for Cochin. On the flight Swamiji told me, "Even if others do not behave in a nice manner, I expect you to be always equanimous, balanced, and discriminating. Equanimity and balance of mind is yoga,

Ravindra and I attending Swamiji's yagna, May 1973, Bangalore, India

as stated in the second chapter of the Geeta: *samatvam yoga uchayate."*

Swamiji said, "At all times, try to be balanced and smiling. Be like a flower, fragrant and smiling. Use your thorns only when someone tries to pluck you out from the roots." He paused and then continued, "Have an ideal and stick to it. A vedantic teacher will only show the light to you. You have to live your own path." These words touched me deeply and have stayed with me since.

Swamiji's words acted as an *upadesha vakya*, a special instruction based on the scriptures given to a student, which is helpful for her spiritual growth. I began to understand that this balance and equipoise which I have always nurtured in my heart, is the essence of life.

I came to this realization much later, in 1992, when I told Swamiji, "The ultimate result of all this knowledge and teaching is being peaceful and balanced in all circumstances."

During all the years of my association with Swamiji I discovered some of his favorite verses from the Bhagavad Geeta. They are listed in the notes at the end of the book[1].

May 23, 1973

From Cochin we proceeded to Trivandrum where Swamiji was scheduled to give a talk at a Balvihar children's program. Thousands of children were expected to attend. Swamiji created the Balvihar program which are weekly classes for children. Here they would learn culture and traditional values through storytelling as well as music, art, dance and drama.

It was at this function that I spoke in front of a large audience for the very first time. It was not easy, but with Swamiji's grace I managed it pretty well for a first attempt. Swamiji and I were on the dais at the same time and I really wanted to have a photograph taken as a momento of the event. It was disappointing when the photographer failed to show up.

Shylja Menon, a devotee also traveling with Swamiji, taught me a Malayalam song called *Cheti Mandaram Tulsi*, honoring Lord Guruvayurappa, who appears in the form of baby Krishna. This song describes the offering of *tulsi* (holy basil) garlands, *mandar* and jasmine flowers to the deity. Swamiji sang along. It was a memorable moment hearing my Guru sing. He adored Lord Guruvayurappa. Later Swamiji took me for darshan to the Guruvayur Temple which is one of the most famous holy pilgrimage centers for devotees of Lord Krishna.

Our trip to South India was nearing its end, and we were to fly back to Bombay from Cochin. There were no vacant chairs in the airport waiting area so Swamiji calmly went and sat on the steps of the porch. I sat down near him. Suddenly, the Rani of Cochin (the queen of the state and a relative of Swamiji's sister) arrived and was horrified to see Swamiji sitting on the steps. She immediately invited him to join her in the V.I.P. lounge. There he sat with the same equipoise as he had sat in the verandah thereby teaching me in practice the meaning of the words, 'balance is yoga' (samatvam yoga uchyate).

May 31, 1973
Bombay to Poona

Shubhra and I accompanied Swamiji to Poona. It was a memorable drive with all of us singing bhajans and other songs. Swamiji especially liked a song called *Yeh kya hua* from the movie *Amar Prem*, whose meaning translates to: "What has happened, how has this happened, when did this happen?" Swamiji said, "The meaning is full of Vedanta. All thoughts which make a seeker wonder about creation and his role in it are vedantic."

During the drive back to Bombay I seized the opportunity to share some of my reflections with Swamiji. I asked,

"Swamiji, any act of love can take place only when the doer feels a sense of identity towards the object of his or her love. If the identification is merely at the level of body, mind or intellect, then there is a problem because the body and its conditions, moods, and ideas go on changing in both the lover and the loved. When a person truly loves another, then he or she identifies with them at all levels - physical, mental, intellectual and spiritual. So my question is that in order to avoid any problems, should love be identification only at the spiritual or consciousness level of the self? This is a dilemma to me."

Swamiji answered, "No, love should be total identification at all levels. The cause of trouble is not identification, but attachment. We should not get attached. For example if we identify with a cause, say women's independence or equality. We identify with it intellectually, but we should not get attached. We should not feel that the cause only belongs to me. I, who am connected with it, am not alone. A large number of people in the world are also connected with that cause. So this identification is with an attitude which is not egocentric. The expression of this love is at all levels: body, mind and intellect; as well as with the source of oneness, which is the One Atman or Self."

I asked Swamiji for clarification on another point. "Every religion and book on ethics says 'help others'. What does 'other' mean to a vedantin? She knows that the truth is the same

'Self' in everyone. What is conceived or perceived as 'other' is the body-mind-intellect (BMI) equipment which itself is an illusion. Maybe the only help the Vedantin can offer is to give the knowledge of the true Self to others. Is that all?"

Swamiji answered, "Right."

I asked, "Swamiji, is helping at the body-mind-intellect level also important?"

Swamiji replied, "Yes, because we are living in an illusion ourselves, we do consider the body-mind-intellect complex as real. We have to help others by identifying with them at all levels until one realizes the truth that everything is considered an illusion. With the help of the scriptural text the teacher then can remove this illusion."

JUNE 1, 1973
SWAMIJI'S WORLD TOUR

The evening before leaving on his world tour, Swamiji handed me a piece of paper. Clearly outlined were some instructions that I was to follow in his absence:

1. Keep the puja room not too cluttered. While meditating sit on the same seat, at the same place, preferably at the same time.

2. Try to help in the work of the mission of the Swami by helping with a manuscript, story writing, or any other work like organizing a yagna.
3. Explain to others what you know about religion, rebirth, values of life and eternal truth in order to make them interested in something higher. But never get excited, even with one who speaks against the Swami or religion. Hear everything calmly and with a smile. Don't speak much. Understand fully, then in few words try to explain or express your viewpoint. Don't get excited.
4. In order to tell others about spiritual life you should read as per the scheme of study written in *Kindle Life* (text on the fundamentals of Vedanta). In slow, small doses absorb, digest and assimilate.
5. The main thing is that others will appreciate more if you practice the thoughts in your daily life. Be cheerful, have equanimity of the mind, be poised under all circumstances and serve others. Give them love and sacrifice for them. Make every act in life a picture of beauty, expressing the truth given out in our religion. Make the whole life and all experiences a smiling orchestra, blending in harmony, spreading cheer.
6. See the good points, the better aspect of every person and situation.

7. Life is a tragedy to those who feel and a comedy to those who think.
8. Don't just blabber or speak unnecessary words. Know your mind and put it in a concise and clear manner in speech.

These simple words of Swamiji contain the essential values for spiritual living and are useful to all seekers.

When asked about his return to India, Swamiji said, "I'll be back soon." I thought to myself that 'soon' is a relative term. He told me not to go into the formalities of wishing him a pleasant journey but to mean it in the heart only.

Swamiji instructed me to work for the Chinmaya Mission in Ahmedabad while he was away. I was also to continue my study of Vedanta. He asked me if I could join him in Canada and the United States during his tour. I told him I would try and would know better after I got his itinerary.

That night Preeta, Vinita and I hardly slept. We stayed up all night talking about Swamiji. During the pre-dawn drive to the airport Swamiji told us he knew we had been talking about him.

August, 1973
USA trip

Swamiji and I exchanged many letters. My plan worked out well and I did go to USA at the end of August. I stayed with my sister Preeta and her husband Gopal Kapoor at their home in Allentown, Pennsylvania about sixty miles from Philadelphia.

September 2, 1973
Philadelphia

When Swamiji arrived in Philadelphia I picked him up at the airport. It was almost too good to be true! The drive back to Allentown presented a rare and perfect opportunity for me to discuss many things with Swamiji; most of the time he was surrounded by devotees. We conversed in Hindi.

Swamiji had cardiac problems and diabetes, but in spite of these health issues he always remained cheerful. He told me, "You don't know your real beauty. See yourself with my eyes." He was speaking of my true Self. In every word of his there was an indication to me to turn towards the spiritual reality.

Swamiji stayed at Preeta and Gopal's house. Every morning he would drink his tea sitting on the patio, facing the picturesque view of the mountains. At times he would sit there while responding to the thick bundle of mail that he would receive daily. He taught me how to open an envelope neatly. Swamiji told me that every action, even the smallest ones, should be done with perfection. It must have the stamp of excellence.

Preeta is an excellent cook and she would make a variety of dishes every day. Wanting to please Swamiji I attempted to prepare *Gujarati kadhi*, a kind of soup, for him. It didn't turn out very well but he tasted it and just smiled and said, "I really can't finish this, although my Guru did eat the *khichdi* that I made even though it was not cooked properly. That was his greatness."

Later on, I practiced cooking the kadhi with devotion. I would think of Sri Annapoorna Devi, the goddess of food, while cooking and the end result would be perfect. Swamiji always enjoyed it and often asked me to make it for him.

OCTOBER, 1973
CAMBRIDGE, MASSACHUSETTS
MASSACHUSETTS INSTITUTE OF TECHNOLOGY

Swamiji was invited to MIT to give a series of talks. We stayed in an apartment for visiting professors on the campus. There was an amazing view of the Charles River and the city of Boston from this penthouse apartment. The river glistened in the sun and sailboats traced patterns on the water. The beautiful panorama unfolding before us set the mood for the talks to come. The eternal sunshine of Swamiji's radiance and warmth illumined my mind.

Not being accustomed to daily cooking and cleaning without any help, I did my best to look after Swamiji and cook for him. I prepared sandwiches, soups and *upama*, a breakfast food made with cream of wheat, vegetables and spices. I would supplement his meals with fresh fruits, juices and buttermilk. He graciously ate whatever I offered him. Later on Swamiji would joke about my cooking by saying, "She always kept me hungry."

Early in the morning, around 4:30 a.m. I would hear Swamiji lovingly call out my name "Neee..ruuu," outside my bedroom door, to wake me up.

Once, while I was busy preparing to serve lunch, Swamiji came into the kitchen and started stirring yogurt to make buttermilk. This was not something one would expect to see from a Swami; he was one of a kind! On another occasion when I was removing the dishes from the dinner table Swamiji began peeling an apple. He ate some and then cut the rest for me saying, "Now eat." I will never forget those small but affectionate gestures of love.

Our days were long and we worked continuously from 5 a.m. until 10 p.m. One night I was especially tired. Swamiji gently patted my back and blessed me as I did my pranams to him. Immediately all of my pain and fatigue faded away.

Swamiji would shower me with his unconditional love and give me the rare opportunity of his seva. How can I be worthy to be near him, I wondered?

Once Swamiji said to me, "You are pure gold." Later in a discourse He explained that the *sakshi atman*, the pure consciousness that is the witness of everything within, is like twenty-four carat pure gold. It is mixed with other metals (vasanas) and shaped in various forms of ornaments which are the body, mind, intellect equipment. When we remove the impurities by the heat of *gyana*, *tapasya*, and *upasana* (knowledge, penance and worship), the gold regains its pure nature. In this same way, when we detach from the impurities of the body, mind and intellect we realize the one sakshi atman within, which is like pure gold.

During my stay in Cambridge there were times when I missed my children and felt a bit guilty about leaving them with my mother. Swamiji would console me by saying, "The best way you can help the children is to pray for them with all your heart and devotion, wherever you are. You cannot be physically with them all of the time. Sometimes parents have to travel and be away from their children. Your intentions here are good. You have come for satsang, not to be entertained or to shop around. Your love and prayers will make the Lord protect them and give them strength, wherever they are."

This advice has been of great help to me, whenever I had to be away from my children. I feel that sincere prayers for our children always help to protect them during difficult times.

Swamiji once said, "As you feel about your beloved children, I feel for my beloved *sruti* (vedas)." I asked him, "Have any of your disciples or followers attained God realization?" He answered, "No one yet."

In Cambridge, Mimi Robbins, Sheela Kripalani, Mrs. Nirula, my cousin Poonam and her husband Narendra Patni, were among the many devotees who came regularly for the discourses and also invited Swamiji for bhiksha. Gopal Rangaswamy used to drive Swamiji to all the lectures. His parents also attended Swamiji's lectures and were among the founders of the Chinmaya Mission in India.

Every day at dawn, Swamiji would give a discourse on *Kena Upanishad*. His words transported us to the Himalayas, to the ancient hermitage of the *rishis* (masters) near the river Ganga. His evening talk was on the Bhagavad Geeta, chapter III, which reinforced what I had learned while in Bangalore.

Kena Upanishad presents a beautiful exposition of the ultimate reality, the truth within ourselves, which the teacher expresses in reply to a question from the disciple:

> *"By whom willed and directed does the mind light upon its object? Commanded by whom does the main vital air (prana) proceed to function? By whose will do men utter speech? What intelligence directs the eyes and the ears (towards their respective objects)?"*

The teacher replies:

> *"It is the ear of the ear, the mind of the mind, the speech of speech, the vital air of the vital air, and the eye of the eye. The wise, freeing themselves and rising above the senses, become immortal."*

These two verses are well known to all students of Vedanta. The mystical literature of the Upanishads is written in an inimitable and cryptic style. Our attention is directed to that which is behind our senses and the mind: the very light of consciousness, by which all these instruments are illumined. In the study of the Upanishads words alone are not important. Swamiji said, "The Upanishadic teaching in order to be effective has to be heard directly from the mouth of the guru. The Self is the eternal 'knower' of all that is known as well as all that is not known. One who knows this, he alone comprehends it."

The essence of the Upanishad was elaborated by Swamiji. He said, "As our head and heart soak in it, both these wings carry us high towards 'That' bliss, peace and silence."

Ravindra arrived in Cambridge one week later and together we traveled to Montreal, Canada without Swamiji.

Our next visit with Swamiji was in New York, at the home of a devotee. Ravindra and I had traveled one hundred miles by taxi to see Swamiji. He was unwell with a fever and a bad cough. And yet he was still smiling, always glad to see us. We were able to spend only one hour with him before leaving for our flight back to India. Swamiji asked us, "Why did you take so much trouble and spend so much money just to meet me for one hour?" I told him "Swamiji, it is more than worth it, just to have your darshan!"

Powai, December, 1973

DECEMBER 1973
POWAI, BOMBAY

I SPENT THE DAY AT POWAI, attending classes and doing *swadhyaya* (study). In the evening Swamiji was sitting in his usual spot on the terrace in front of the temple. Aubrey Menon came to meet Swamiji and thanked him for agreeing to be interviewed and allowing ashram activities to be photographed. Aubrey Menon was writing a book called *The New Mystics*. He was an agnostic writer who had already written a book on the Ramayana. Swamiji referring to it, lashed out at Menon in his inimitable style, "It was a vomit of your intellect." Swamiji then explained the mystical meaning of Ramayana:

> "Lord Rama represents the Pure Consciousness. Sita the mind. Lakshman the *jiva* (ego). When Sita starts desiring the world of objects as represented by the golden deer, she is helplessly carried away by the ten senses represented by the demon King Ravana. This separation from her source, her real self, makes her sorrowful. Later, Hanuman representing *tapasya* (penance), *seva* (service), *brahmacharya* (chastity), comes to the assistance of Sita and gives her a message from

Rama. Assured by this messenger, she waits until the ten-headed Ravana is vanquished by Lord Rama who represents the power of the Self. Finally she reunites with her beloved husband Rama."

Months later, I was pleasantly surprised to see the book *The New Mystics* with a very logical and positive write up about Swami Chinmayananda, describing him as one of the foremost genuine Vedanta teachers of our time. There was a photo in the book taken at the Powai ashram of Swamiji laughing and of me, walking with him but just a step behind. Swamiji was in his kutiya when I showed him the book and the photo. He said to all the people sitting there, "This is a result of her *upasana*."

'Up' means near, 'asana' means to sit. Upasana means mentally stationed near the truth or the guru. Swami Dayananda, who was sitting there said, "She is great." Actually, I never thought that I was doing any upasana, but at the time my mind was totally immersed in devotion and prayers toward my guru, Swami Chinmayananda.

December 1973
Enroute from Bombay to Delhi

On our flight to Delhi the cabin was very hot. I started fanning us with a magazine. Swamiji said, "Learn to bear some heat, have *titiksha* (forbearance), don't continue to fan." I stopped and tried to explain that I was trying to make him more comfortable, "Whenever I sit in a car or plane the sun is on my side, but now it is shining on you." Swamiji answered, "When you are with me you'll always remain in my shadow, but when you are alone, then the sunlight will be on you." He always responded in a manner that required the student to reflect on the deeper meaning of his words.

December 29, 1973
Delhi

Ravindra and I spent the entire day with Swamiji. Sri Satya Sai Baba, the famous saint from South India, also happened to be in Delhi. In the morning we attended his lecture on *The Story of Vasanas*. During the afternoon Swamiji came to our room at the Oberoi Hotel to rest. In the evening we waited outside the room where Swamiji was in a meeting with Sri Satya Sai Baba. Subsequently Swamiji invited us inside, asked us to sit next to him, and offered us prasad from his plate.

January and February, 1974

Swamiji stayed intermittently in Bombay during this period. On the day after Shivaratri, Swamiji talked about the Temple of Bharat, named after Rama's brother in the epic Ramayana. This temple was in Irinjalakuda, Kerala, South India. There were plans to have the *dhwaja pataka* (flag pole) plated in gold. He wanted a few of us to make an offering of some of the gold jewelry we were wearing at the time. I took off my gold earrings. My impertinence made me ask, "Why, when there is so much poverty, should one use gold for such a purpose?" Swamiji explained, "These things are relative, why do we wear expensive ornaments?" I felt ashamed for asking. He crushed the earrings in front of me, silently telling me to crush my ego. I thought, 'I am ready, please do so Lord.'

Several months later Swamiji blessed me by taking me to that temple in Irinjalakuda. I stood inside silently praying, "O Lord, please have Swamiji's lotus feet imprinted in my heart forever." Swamiji completed the *pradakshina* (circumambulation) of the temple at that very moment. As I slowly opened my eyes I saw him standing right in front of me. It was like an instantaneous fulfillment of my prayer. Swamiji said, "Whenever you remember me, I will immediately be present in front of you."

MARCH 1–7, 1974
LUCKNOW

WHEN I TOLD MY MOTHER that Swamiji would be conducting a three-day talk series in Lucknow, she was worried about not having enough strength to help me prepare for it. My mother was recovering from recent cardiac problems and had other medical conditions as well. Her concern was resolved when two of her friends, Kamala Bhargava and Kanta Wahal, volunteered to help me.

I had offered to take care of all the expenses for the talks but Swamiji said a firm "No." He added, "You pay for the air and train tickets and the promotional flyers. As far as the rest of the expenses are concerned, you should go out as my disciple and request people to contribute in the yagna spirit. We should take from them whatever they offer." By yagna spirit he meant the spirit of cooperation as enumerated in the Geeta.

Lucknow, the city of Nawabs, is steeped in history and culture. The Nawabs were Muslim rulers of certain princely states in India. Lucknow is not a city of industry with unlimited wealth. We collected small amounts of money and somehow managed to arrange the first lecture series of Swamiji to be held in here.

When my brother Peush heard that Swamiji was coming to Lucknow, he told me, "I am not interested in all this religious talk about swamis." But after much pleading from me, he agreed to attend. "I will stay for only one lecture and then leave for Bombay."

When we finally arrived in Lucknow, Peush and his wife Nelu, Shubhra and about fifteen other devotees were waiting to receive Swamiji at the railway station with garlands in hand. More people were waiting for him at my parent's house, where he met my mother for the first time.

On this first visit we arranged a discourse by Swamiji on the *Logic of Spirituality* at the Carlton Hotel. His talk was a totally modern approach to religion based on logic and not on rituals or superstition. It was very well received and this first lecture series was a great success.

After hearing Swamiji speak, Peush cancelled his trip to Bombay and stayed back in Lucknow. He became Swamiji's driver, transporting him to all of the talks and even cleaning out Swamiji's car!

My sister-in-law Nelu, who is from the Sikh faith, was also quite sceptical about swamis. She ultimately ended up going to all the evening discourses and served Swamiji with great respect. Gradually their friends started coming to hear Swamiji speak as well.

I invited my friend Dr. Birendra Kumar, owner of the Clarks Group of Hotels, to join us for one of Swamiji's talks. He enjoyed it so much that he canceled his business trip to Delhi and stayed back to attend the entire lecture series. Later on he and his family served Swamiji in many ways, offering free use of the hotel space; arranging bhikshas and programs for the Chinmaya Mission.

I would clean and prepare Swamiji's room and make his breakfast. Typically it would be coffee, idli, coconut chutney, fruits, almonds and sometimes toast. He also liked *gujarati chivda* (puffed rice snack) and *tilgud revdi* (a sesame and jaggery candy) which is a speciality of Lucknow. Again he teased me about my hopeless cooking. I offered him pomegranate seeds from my cupped palm and as he ate he told me about four different types of *mukti* or liberation:

1. *Sayujya* - the experience of being one or merging with the Lord.
2. *Samipya* - closeness to the Lord.
3. *Salokya* - dwelling in the same abode as the Lord.
4. *Saroopya* - being as the same form as the Lord.

Relaxing in the winter sun in my family home. Lucknow 1974

Every morning, while at my mother's house, we enjoyed satsang with Swamiji in a very informal atmosphere. Leela Nambiar, an ardent devotee of Swamiji from Chennai, was also in Lucknow to attend the lectures. He invited her and some others to join him on his visit to Uttarkashi. I foolishly asked him, "Why don't you relax alone? Why do you call everyone to join you?" Swamiji replied, "So that they can also get the benefit of satsang." Behind the simplicity of these words lay a profound teaching.

During his visit Swamiji met some classmates from Lucknow University. This was his alma mater where he had completed a double major in English Literature and Law from 1940 to 1942. He talked about going to jail as a freedom fighter during India's struggle for independence from the British and later working as a sub-editor in the famous newspaper *The National Herald*. He recalled how he went to Rishikesh to interview Swami Sivananda of the Divine Life Society. His aim was to write an exposé about the fantastic claims of Hindu ancient texts and religious masters and prove that they were charlatans. Instead, Swamiji was so convinced about the greatness of the spiritual way of life that he took sanyasa in 1949 from Swami Sivananda. He then went to Uttarkashi for intense study of the ancient Vedanta texts, the Upanishads, Bhagavad Geeta and Brahma Sutras. Swamiji continued his studies with the renowned renunciate saint and scholar, Swami

Tapovan Maharaj, who lived on the banks of the Ganga near Gangotri and Uttarkashi.

During his stay in Lucknow, Swamiji watched our gardener lovingly tend to all the plants. The garden was in full bloom with roses, dahlias, petunias and other winter flowers. Swamiji said, "The gardener is a real karma yogi. He works with total concentration, dedicated to his goal."

One night while returning from yagna and bhiksha, Swamiji saw the watchman sitting in the verandah with a lantern. He was chanting the *Tulsi Ramayana* with great devotion. Swamiji blessed him and commented to us, "These are the majority of the people in India. It is because of their devotion and simplicity, India still survives."

While having breakfast one day Swamiji noticed a photograph of my late father, Prem Narain Tandon, hanging in the dining room. I started to talk about my father's enthusiasm for life and studies and concluded sadly, "He is no more." Swamiji immediately intervened and said, "Never say 'he is no more.' He has left his body, but he is still here. He was a great spiritual seeker, very regular in his sadhana, which he did quietly." I wondered how Swamiji could have known so much about my father, from one photo.

During another conversation with Swamiji, I said, "I just go on like a……". "Automaton," Swamiji finished my sentence. On another occasion, when I must have been taunting someone, Swamiji told me, "You are a zero, an automaton. Keep your taunting arrows inside your purse." He then suggested that I do some social work. At the time I didn't like this idea at all. I thought only of my personal self-improvement on the path of spirituality. Now I know better. As one grows within, one's spiritual roots become stronger. The individual blossoms into a full-grown tree which provides a resting-place for all who come under its shelter.

MAY, 1974
BOMBAY

SWAMIJI WAS INSPECTING a new hall being built near his kutiya when I arrived at the ashram. I did pranams and said to him, "It seems we are mad," referring to all of our frequent visits to Powai.

He answered, "Let this madness increase a thousand fold. Let this tree grow, don't kill it. Let it blossom, let the branches and flowers increase. Don't compare yourself with anyone." This was good advice; otherwise negative tendencies can develop and get in the way of getting the maximum benefit of the guru's grace.

Later in the day Swamiji also advised me, "Try to leave the support of the guru, time, place, conducive environment. Take his help, but go out and practice."

The holy saint Sri Ma Anandamayi

May, 1974
Meeting Sri Ma Anandamayi
Andheri, Bombay

*M*a Anandamayi is regarded as one of the most exalted God-realized saints of the twentieth century. Her devotees ranged from Prime Ministers to monks to simple villagers. People came from all over the world just to see her and sit in her presence. Her face radiated peace and brilliance and she had an incredible aura of spiritual grace.

Though she hardly had a formal education, she spoke authoritatively on the direct experience of God.

I recall that in 1973, after my darshan of Ma and Swamiji together in the Powai temple, Swamiji said, "I will take you with me to hear Ma speak." He kept that promise, but in a very odd way.

One day while I was at the ashram, Swamiji suddenly disappeared. Wondering where he was going and wanting to be near him, I followed him in my car to a building in the suburbs. It turned out he was on his way to Andheri to meet Ma Anandamayi for the installation of a *Radha Krishna* idol. I entered the hall with a bit of trepidation and when I saw him, he was already seated at Ma's side. He noticed me and called out my name. For me, it was a dream of a lifetime to sit so close to Swamiji and Ma. I went to the front of the room and sat down directly facing them. They were smiling at each other with love and respect. They conversed in Hindi:

Swamiji said, "Ma we are late." (Swamiji was always punctual, hence the apology).

Ma responded, "Whenever you come, it is the right time."

Ma said to her host, "Please receive him and honor him."

Ma asked Swamiji, "Will you come every day?"

"Yes, Ma, I will give a talk each evening."

Ma, while looking at Swamiji, spoke to everyone in the room, "See all of you, *gyana amrita* (the nectar of knowledge) will flow from Baba's *shreemukh* (mouth). Receive it on your forehead and be blessed."

Swamiji gently responded, "All of these devotees have come for your darshan Ma, not for me." I was smiling when Ma called me closer to her.

After the meeting was over I escorted Swamiji to his car and returned to find Ma sitting in the verandah. She asked me, "Has Baba gone?"

I answered "Yes Ma" and offered my pranams to her. She said to me, "Come again." Ma's words, spoken so sweetly, did come true. Six months later, in December of 1974, at Ma's ashram, Naimisharanya, I had the opportunity to hear her speak again. I felt blessed.

June 7, 1974

Swamiji came to Worli for the dedication of a new art school for children. A senior devotee, Pushpa Jaisinghani, was running the Chinmaya Nursery School as well as Kalamandir, an art center. Ravindra had helped raise funds for the school and Swamiji was very grateful to him. I had the feeling he was not giving the rest of us credit for all our hard work. Most likely, Swamiji didn't want us to develop *ahamkara* (ego) for contributing to the school.

I mentioned this to Ram Batra who agreed with me saying, "Being with Swamiji is like being caught in a lion's paw." Ram Batra was speaking from experience and wisdom which could only come from being one of the closest devotees of Swamiji. I later read in Ramana Maharshi's book that it is the guru's job, like a lion, to kill the elephant ego of the disciple.

September, 1974
Calcutta

*S*wamiji went to Calcutta for a yagna. Wanting a much needed break from my daily routine I went to visit him for a few days. I stayed with Mrs. Bhargava who was also hosting Swamiji. I had little opportunity to spend time alone with him but Swamiji's discourses made my trip worthwhile. They were like nectar to my tired soul. His very presence was a magic balm for me.

During the morning discourse on *Kaivalya Upanishad*, I found my mind becoming totally attentive and tuned to Swamiji's words. I glided into another dimension of consciousness. I became completely silent and still.

After the lecture Swamiji remarked, "Really, it has happened? Neeru, silent? I am giving heavy doses of sattwic vibrations because you are here only for a few days."

A young boy asked Swamiji, "Why this path?" He smiled and replied, "I have found this full of happiness. I am always open, if you can show and convince me of a better way, I'll take it."

During a breakfast bhiksha at Mr. B. K. Birla's house, his wife, Sarla Birla, served us food with great affection and brought us apples saying, "These are from our apple orchards in Kullu." Swamiji softly said, "God's garden." Sarlaji smiled and said, "Yes Swamiji."

Swamiji liked the Sattwin trees in our host's garden. They had white fragrant bud like flowers. When I mentioned to Swamiji that it would be a good idea to plant some of these trees in the ashram he agreed and asked me to get them. We planted them behind the Jagadeeshwara Temple in Powai, Bombay and in 1999, I was delighted to see that three out of the original five trees were still flourishing, tall and beautiful.

My aunt Manju Rai had invited Swamiji and a few of us to her home for bhiksha. She lived in Baranagore, a short drive from Calcutta. Her house was a beautiful colonial bungalow on the banks of the river Hooghly, the local name for the river Ganga. On the opposite bank was Belur Math the spiritual center of the Ramakrishna Mission. The family that lived on the ground floor of my aunt's house had been following the teachings of Swamiji but had never met him. They had a large picture of Swamiji in their living room. The husband, who had recently passed away, had wanted very much to meet Swamiji and invite him home. You can imagine the joy his wife felt when Swamiji decided to visit her briefly. He told the elderly widow, "*Amma* (mother), I will come and stay here for a month; don't tell anyone."

Swamiji asked my aunt Manju and my friend Damayanti Kapoor, "Do you see any change in Neeru?" When they answered "Yes," Swamiji replied, "Yes, there is very little change; it is a painful growth." I wanted to hear more, but somehow the subject got changed.

On the spiritual path one has to swallow bitter pills; but the bitterness somehow seems to always have a sweet aftertaste. It is as if the bitter-coated pill has a honey-filled center. Swamiji would keep me at a distance but soothe me from within. Maybe these are the growing pains that he spoke of. Swamiji told the others how, for many months, I would commute to Powai every day both in the morning and evening, just to hear his discourses on the ancient holy texts. When we were alone I told Swamiji, "You just kill the person." He answered, "I destroy to rebuild."

Swamiji gave all of his disciples the 'ego-treatment'. First he would encourage the disciples, allowing them to feel close to him. When the disciples' ego became inflated he would ignore them completely, thereby deflating their ego. It is the job of a guru to see that the individual ego of the disciple is eliminated, while confidence in their true Self is increased. This process goes on until the ego merges into the Supreme Self.

On the day I was to return to Bombay, Swamiji said to me, "You never come, you never go." With these six words he directed my mind to the eternal nature of my being.

October, 1974
Powai Ashram

Swamiji taught us the spiritual way of life in everything that he did; from discourses on the scriptures to interacting with people and managing such a vast organization. I often watched Swamiji going through the accounts of the Tara Cultural Trust which managed the ashram. He would ask the manager for a detailed expense of various items including milk. He said, "This money is given in trust by people and even a small amount should not be wasted."

Swamiji was also very particular about issuing receipts from the main organization, Central Chinmaya Mission Trust for any donations received.

Once we had an interesting discussion on faith, including the Jain and Vaishnava philosophies as well as other schools of religious thought. Swamiji said, "All efforts in the spiritual field are for nurturing and stabilizing faith. Ultimately one reaches the supreme faith unshaken and waits at the door of Truth. It is only the Almighty by whose grace the door can open anytime." This faith, when directed single pointedly towards God, is called *sharanagati* or surrender to God.

October, 6, 1974
Bombay

Bhartiya Vidya Bhavan, an institute for Indian Culture, was the perfect environment for Swamiji's discourses. The focus of his talk was the famed text *Vivekachoodamani* by Adi Shankaracharya, which translates to *The Crest Jewel of Discrimination*. The following day Swamiji took me completely by surprise when he handed me a certificate for the Vedanta Lesson Course. Hamirbhai Vissanji, a Trustee of Chinmaya Mission who was in charge of the course, told me, "You are the only disciple to whom Swamiji has personally handed the certificate." I thought, God alone knows why I have the good fortune of being blessed by His infinite grace. He is an ocean of compassion, always forgiving our faults and weaknesses. We only have to surrender to Him, with an open heart.

While driving back to the ashram, one of Swamiji's oldest devotees said, "Swamiji you gave the same discourse on *Vivekachoodamani* that you have been giving for the past twenty years. Swamiji patted his back saying, "*Shabash* (bravo), this means I have been consistent. Truth is one. How can it's description be changed? Sometimes, during a discourse, one may change a few illustrations in accord with the modern scientific atmosphere."

Someone asked Swamiji, "In order to receive the Lord's grace what effort did Arjuna's wife Draupadi and Gajendra, the God of the elephants make? Lord Vishnu saved them when they were in trouble." Swamiji replied, "Self surrender is the effort to be made."

Later Swamiji said, "You don't know what I know. Grace is there, but a guru is not genuine if he says it is his."

Swamiji soon made me realize the grace of the guru when he pleasantly surprised me by visiting our home. He came with two of his senior devotees on October 11 to bless me and wish me a happy birthday.

October 19, 1974

Swamiji graced our home in Worli Sea Face, Bombay with a visit. We received him in the formal way, with *poorna kumbha* (ceremonial welcome given to a spiritual master), *chandan* (sandalwood), *kesar tilak* (saffron paste on the forehead) and floral garlands. We chanted vedic mantras while performing aarti. Smiling, he said, "It's the same old Swami, why all this?" My sister-in-law Vinita stood holding a bowl of fruit. Swamiji said to her, "So, you want fruit?" Later that evening Swamiji blessed Vinita and her husband, Arvind. Shortly after Vinita became pregnant.

By the grace of Swamiji we had organized a satsang at my home. Approximately two hundred people attended. Purshottam Jalota, a famous singer, sang the most uplifting bhajans. Swamiji gave a short talk on *True Religion and Spirituality*. He explained that although we know theoretically about religion, we do not see its effects in daily life.

Proficiency means having knowledge based on studies or observation, much as a professor who knows all about electricity but may not be able to repair a damaged wire effectively.

Efficiency is the art of applying that knowledge in day-to-day situations in order to achieve maximum results by minimum expenditure of energy. This is achieved by practice and by removing the obstacles that block our ability to perform. For example, water in a tank on the roof of a building may not come out of a tap on a lower floor because there is a blockage somewhere in the pipe. An efficient person would know how to remove the blockage and let the water flow.

In the same way, the knowledge acquired through study is stored in the brain but with certain people it manifests at the right time through their actions or reactions. The mental disturbances or blockages can be of three types:

1. Any negative memories of the past felt as sorrow or anger in the heart.

2. Anxieties for the uncertainty of the future, which are experienced as worries in the mind.
3. Excitement or wavering in the present.

One who is not affected by any of the above and has the knowledge to act in the right way is able to accomplish his work. The time-tested way to remove these obstacles is called yoga.

During the satsang, Swamiji asked me to sing his favorite bhajan which was also a favorite of my grandfather's.

Magan Ishwar ki bhakti mein arre man kyon nahin hota.
Pada aalasya mein murakh rahega kab talak sota?

Oh, my mind and heart why don't you immerse yourself in devotion? Why are you lazy when you know that no relationship in this world lasts forever except the true relationship with the Lord, who is all-knowing, all-pervading and eternal?

After having a meal together, all the guests were given prasad and a book written by Swamiji called *Kindle Life*. Swamiji was very pleased with the way the evening went.

October 24, 1974
Powai Ashram

*V*IJAYADASHMI IS AN IMPORTANT Hindu festival. On this day Swamiji gave me his blessings by gifting me a rare gold coin and saying, "Multiply and increase." In appreciation I had a gold box engraved with an *Om* symbol and presented it to him. He told me it was small for his hand. It was, but I'm sure his point was that I should not get caught up with material gifts. It could increase the ego.

October 26, 1974

*S*WAMIJI WAS FLYING TO JAMSHEDPUR for a National Yagna. In the car on the way to the airport, he gave me as prasad, a beautiful *rudraksha* ring set in copper and gold. Rudraksha is the dried fruit from the sacred tree of the same name. Considered to be full of healing and divine properties, it is usually used in a rosary for *japa* (repetition of a mantra). I was reminded of the time that Swamiji showed me a necklace that he was wearing made of double rudraksha beads which is called *Gaurishankar*. It had been presented to him by the pontiff of the Shankaracharya Sringeri Mutt,

Sri Chandrasekhar Bharti III. This *Mutt* (center) is one of four that were established in the eighth and ninth century by the great philosopher Adi Shankaracharya. Swamiji belongs to the Saraswati lineage of the Sringeri Mutt and it was an honor for him to receive this necklace.

Swamiji said, "It is a token representing intelligence, given by the current Shankaracharya; therefore the Swami should wear it."

December, 1974
Bombay

On December 1st Swamiji returned to India from his South East Asia trip. I went to meet him in Powai. He asked me "Why do you look so sad? I drop those who don't improve. *Hum chola chod denge, phir nahin lenge.*" His words in Hindi meant: This time I'll leave this body and will not take it up again.

That night I couldn't stop my tears. During meditation I prayed to Swamiji, "If you think I am worthy of getting your blessings, then take me to Trichur with you." Earlier, Swamiji had promised to take me to Guruvayur which is a short drive from Trichur. The travel plans were vague and had not yet been confirmed.

Miraculously my prayer was answered. On a fully booked and oversold flight one seat became available. I jumped at the opportunity and the next morning joined Swamiji at the airport. Swamiji was not at all surprised to see me. He referred to knowing about my prayer to him last night. "Oh, how stupid of me," I thought. "When will I know him as the *antaryamin*, the all-knowing one! He knows the thoughts of those who have surrendered to him."

DECEMBER 1974
TRIP TO COCHIN, ERNAKULAM, TRICHUR, AND GURUVAYUR
ON THE PLANE TO SOUTH INDIA

THE FLIGHT ATTENDANT offered Swamiji a cup of coffee and a snack but he chose to have only coffee. I had an apple with me which I cut into pieces with the penknife I kept in my purse. I served the apple slices to Swamiji on a paper napkin, being careful to keep the peels on one side of the napkin and the apple slices on the other. I told Swamiji, "I'm sorry for serving you in such an untidy way."

He replied, "It is the *bhava* (feeling) that counts." He then took a slice of apple and continued, "From the highest standpoint, what else is there but dirt all around on the body level? It is the bhava within you, which alone is accepted by the Lord."

After gathering the courage to ask, I said, "Swamiji, how can you see what is going on in our minds?"

He answered, "One can enter the mind of another, but it is not done unless really necessary. The mind is a thousand times more delicate than a flower. It should not be disturbed. What is there to see? All the minds have the same vasanas. It is painful to come down from the highest level of bliss and then function in samsara. Only the most compassionate can do it." I silently thanked Swamiji for his grace.

There were pictures of Krishna and the *gopis* (Krishna's young female devotees) on the cabin walls of the Air India plane. I wondered out aloud, "Where is Radha?" She was the most important among the gopis.

Swamiji answered, "Here with me; the cows were all there in Lucknow, listening to me."

"And the gopis?" I asked.

Swamiji replied with his usual droll humor, "They are coming to the airport to receive me." As always many devotees were at the airport when we arrived.

Radha was the beloved of Lord Krishna. Their union symbolized divine love. Krishna is pure consciousness and Radha his power of love and creation; an expansion of himself. She was the main gopi of Vrindavan. From the realized master's viewpoint, the gopis represent the rishis and vedas, and the thousands of thoughts or *vrittis*, playing with pure consciousness. In total surrender to Him, dependent on Him, they realize pure love and union with the Lord.

From Cochin airport we drove to Ernakulum, the twin city of Cochin and Swamiji's birth place, to visit one of his devotees. In that area there are spice plantations and the beautiful backwaters that Kerala is so famous for. By the time we left to continue our journey to Trichur, a magnificent full moon had risen. It had a reddish glow and Swamiji remarked to me, "When I see this moon with the dark spot, it reminds me of you." I could not comprehend the exact meaning of his words at that time but a year later when I read the *Gospel of Ramakrishna* there was a description of the full red moon. The moon represents bhakti or devotion. It is full and reddish in color and symbolic of the light of knowledge. The dark spots on it represent the vasanas or desires in the mind of the devotee.

In Trichur, Swamiji stayed at a small home near Vivekodyam High School where the yagna was held. As a child Swamiji studied at this same school. I was a guest at the home of Swamiji's childhood friend. I was thrilled to visit Swamiji's ancestral home where he had spent his childhood. He was in a great mood. He enjoyed the home cooked food served on green banana leaves while chatting in the local dialect, Malayalam. The body was nourished by delicious South Indian food, while the mind and intellect with discourses on *Kenopanishad* and chapter XIII of the *Bhagavad Geeta*.

The cultural programs following the evening lecture were a rare treat. In the *Kathakali* form of classical dance, we saw the depiction of the mythical stories. One in particular, depicting the Ramayana, brought tears to Swamiji's eyes.

There were times in which Swamiji remained aloof and silent. It was painful to be so near him yet feel so distant. My eyes often brimmed with tears, but these were tears of inner peace and calm that had descended over me. One evening Swamiji took us to visit a small temple of Ma Bhuvaneshwari Devi (divine mother) and the *navagrahas* (nine planets). After this visit Swamiji expressed that Ravindra and I should donate a *Kalyanmandapam*, wedding hall, for those people who could not afford to rent a venue for their marriage ceremony. It was named 'Neeranjali' by Swamiji meaning 'Neeru's tribute.' I was touched by this honor.

On December 4, we drove through the lush countryside. The emerald green paddy fields, the banana trees and the ponds covered with the lotus flowers were a soothing sight for tired eyes. Nearby was the small village of Kaladi where Adi Shankara grew up. Fifty miles from there is the maternal ancestral home of Adi Shankaracharya and his place of birth. Swamiji acquired this property, restored it and renamed it 'Adi Sankara Nilayam'. He converted it into a research center for Sanskrit and philosophy.

Visiting Sri Guruvayurappa temple with Swamiji was the highlight of my trip. We had a wonderful darshan and were fortunate to accompany the *utsav murti*, a small idol of Lord Krishna, which was placed on an elephant and taken out in a procession. We received special sandalwood paste as prasad. Swamiji had arranged for a twenty-four hour special puja to be performed for us at a later date. I felt that I had already received his blessings in advance.

When we returned to Trichur, we attended a *padapuja* at a devotee's home. Swamiji later said, "You wanted to know how the feet of the guru are worshipped? Padapuja is worshipping the feet of the master. This ritual symbolizes the truth and *tapas* (penance) on which he stands. It is praying to the one non-dual Truth, which appears as many."

I was reluctant to return home after such a memorable trip. I asked Swamiji, "How can we stop the coming and going?" Once again he brought back the focus from the outer to the inner in his cryptic reply, "One who goes, has to come. By 'His Grace' be always in Him."

Performing pada puja (washing the master's feet).
Onlooker is my sister and her son.

December 24, 1974
Naimisharanya
Sri Ma Anandamayi's Ashram

I went with some of my relatives to Naimisharanya, to meet Sri Ma Anandamayi. Swamiji had praised Ma as one of the greatest woman saints of recent times.

Naimisharanya is an ancient pilgrimage center about one hundred miles from my hometown, Lucknow. It remains untouched by commercial development. My uncle had undertaken the task of providing clean and safe drinking water via a tube-well for the pilgrims and devotees who came to visit the Naimisharanya ashram. When we arrived we saw Ma strolling outside in the warm sunlight. My uncle introduced us to her. He mentioned that I had met Ma earlier with Swami Chinmayananda. We all surrounded her as my aunt offered a basket of fruit at her feet. Ma called me close to her. I had brought seedless pomegranates and a hot-water bag as gifts. She lovingly accepted both as I prostrated to her.

Referring to me, my aunt Kusum Rattan remarked, "She has great devotion."

Ma answered, "Yes, she is God's devotee. It is good now you have come to do seva," referring to the tube-well to be made in the ashram.

Ma smiled and led the way to the Veda Purana Mandir. We followed her. Ma praised us when she saw us straightening the cotton carpet which was not evenly spread in the room. We sat near her for a while listening to a Swami as he recited the *Shrimad Bhagavatam*. I was happy to learn later that this Swami had spent time with Pujya Swami Tapovan Maharaj in Uttarkashi. I offered my pranams and a donation. We sang some bhajans while Ma sat smiling silently.

"Why is there so much sorrow in the world?" someone in the group asked. Ma smiled but didn't respond.

My aunt then asked, "Ma, how can we control anger? Sometimes I feel so angry."

Ma answered, "First calm your mind, drink cold water, then take the Lord's name and say: 'Oh God, you came in front of me in this form, I am sorry I got angry, please forgive me, forgive me.'"

My aunt Kusum asked if we could keep the epic book *Mahabharata* in our homes since there was a superstition that if we did, this would lead to fights and conflict in the household.

Ma answered, "It is not so. Many people keep it."

"Living as a householder how do we walk on this path of spirituality?" I asked.

"Why, it is very easy," replied Ma. She instructed me that every time I sat down to meditate, I should invoke the masters or rishis that were connected to my family lineage (*gotra*) with the intention of spiritual growth.

I shared with Ma what Swamiji had once said about her, "Ma, is the most beautiful lady in this world."

Ma just laughed and said something in Bengali, then added in Hindi, "I don't know anything."

"Ma you know everything and you have everything. Please tell us how to become beautiful?" I asked.

"Ask Baba," (meaning Swamiji) she replied. Then Ma said slowly, "*Baba ki aankh lelo*," literally meaning 'Take Baba's vision.' But these words had a deeper meaning: 'Learn from him how to see this world.'

Then, in a louder voice she repeated, "Baba's eyes are beautiful, take them. Just by his mere thought you become a *punyatma*, a *poornatma*" (sacred and fulfilled soul). She meant that we should develop a similar vision to Swamiji who sees everything as auspicious and divine. While reflecting on Ma's words, I longed to develop that inner vision and remembered William Wordsworth's poem, *The Daffodils*:

> ... They flash upon that inward eye
> Which is the bliss of solitude,
> And then my heart with pleasure fills,
> And dances with the daffodils.

In the evening we sat with Ma on the verandah. It was getting cold so I draped a shawl over her shoulders. It was so peaceful to be with her in this sacred place surrounded by lush forests.

February 1, 1975
Powai Ashram

Today I asked Swamiji, "Why do you do all this work of the Mission and ashram? You remain so busy all the time."

Swamiji replied, "The day I 'feel' I am 'doing' I will leave everything. He (God) is 'doing.' I am *akarta* (non-doer) and *abhokta* (non-enjoyer)."

For spiritual aspirants this is one of the crucial concepts they need to master in order to evolve. When a seeker gives up the ego of doer-ship and enjoyer-ship, she operates with a pure heart thereby dissolving all the existing vasanas or karmas.

February 2, 1975

*M*any devotees had brought lunch for Swamiji. He graciously tasted a little from each of the containers, saying, "My *annaprasanam* ceremony must have really been effective."

I asked him, "Where was it done Swamiji?"

He answered, "Near Ernakulam."

Annaprasanam is a ceremony performed when a baby has his first solid food usually at the age of six months. Food is first offered with a prayer to the Lord and then to the baby. The mother or guru makes the child taste all the six varieties of *rasas* or tastes: sweet, sour, salty, bitter, pungent and astringent.

After Swamiji finished his lunch, I stood waiting outside his door for him to retire. When he saw me standing there, he said, "Please turn around and go." When I continued to wait for him to go into his room, he explained, "I cannot close the door on your face." Symbolically a true guru never turns his back on a sincere disciple. This gesture touched my heart.

February 3, 1975

A visitor asked Swamiji about education for Adivasis, tribal people living in the jungles and remote areas. Swamiji answered, "It is enough for them to know *matri devo bhava*: treat mother as God, *pitra devo bhava*: treat father as God, *guru devo bhava*: treat guru as God, and *atithi devo bhava*: treat the guest as God."

Gathering at Neeru's Bombay home with Powai Ashram Brahmacharis in 1975 after their graduation ceremony. Swami Tejomayananda (singing), Swami Purshottamananda and Swami Shantananda are near Neeru.

Swamiji in a joyful meditative mood, listening to bhajans in our Bombay home, 1975.

February 4, 1975
Bombay

Swamiji was sitting with some devotees and telling them all about his Middle East tour. Swamiji counted among his ardent followers people from all nationalities and religious faiths. One such spiritual seeker was from Lebanon. This gentleman, Shaykh Fadhlalla Haeri, would meet Swamiji whenever he could and Swamiji would give him guidance on what to read. Swamiji also told him that he would soon meet a Sufi master who would become his teacher. In time this came to be true. After studying with the Sufi master Shaykh Fadhlalla went on to author several books on Islam, Sufism and the Quran. He had great faith in Swamiji and as a gesture of his appreciation he, along with some others from the Middle East, made a large donation to the Mission.

At the conclusion of his narration Swamiji said,

"The Holy Quran in a way is like Vedanta. It also propagates the principle of one God and the universe as its expression, but the upasana [spiritual practice] methods are different. It is very creditable that some Arabs contributed a large amount of money towards the construction of the main gate at the Jagadeeshwara temple in the Powai ashram. Its consecration is on February 19th. There is an inscription from the Quran on the gate in Arabic, which says, 'Through me pass and go to the Lord of the Universe.'"

My daughter Shreya on Swamiji's lap. Ahmedabad.

February 5, 1975
Powai Ashram

A small group of people accompanied Ravindra and myself to the ashram. Among them were Nita and Mahesh Bhogilal, my sister Rashmi's relatives by marriage. They asked Swamiji, "*Raga* (love) and *dwesha* (hate) are the root of all problems. How should the seeker remain? Knowing all of this, how can he function in a hostile environment and still remain spiritual?"

Swamiji responded, "Who has love and hate? Go above it. Be a *sakshi*, an observer, a mere witness."

The questions continued, "Krishna says that whether one is in the lowest or the highest state of mind, the spiritual urge is always there."

Swamiji explained, "Ninety-eight percent of the people live in imperfection. When they get kicked by nature, some of them change; but the majority do not. For those who are sensitive enough to change, any incident becomes a motivating force to think about and start on their spiritual life." Swamiji continued to explain how this gentleman should continue his *sadhana* (spiritual practice). He should not change his path, his guru or his goal. "Take good advice from everywhere, you are a seeker. Take a few days off for a retreat."

"Swamiji, how do we know whether we are doing correct sadhana or not?"

Swamiji answered, "When our sadhana is wrong, the outward effect is that all the people around become against us; there is tension and no inner joy. But, if the sadhana is done correctly the person starts seeing himself in all those around him. He starts attracting more people. He becomes like a mirror. People will open up to him and feel one with him. Inwardly he is in bliss. Even when difficult situations arise, which would earlier have baffled him, they will no longer upset him. He can stand apart from the situations and still function effectively. Try to find your balance."

February 6, 1975
On the train from Delhi to Lucknow

Swamiji, referring to the true nature of the Self, quoted the following verse from the *Kaivalya Upanishad* in Sanskrit:

> *Na karmana na prajaya, dhanena,*
> *Tyagenaike amritatwamaanshuh.*

> Not by action nor by progeny nor by wealth,
> Only through renunciation, can one reach the immortal state of bliss.

I said, "Swamiji, you are above *sukha-dukha* (joy and sorrow); however, due to our faults and weaknesses we must have given you a lot of pain."

He answered, "No." His eyes were moist and full of love. "Who commits mistakes? Because of the vasanas or *gunas* (the three moods of the mind which correspond to being pure, active and dull), all these things happen. There are innumerable desires which cause us to act and due to the karmic law the result is our prarabdha or destiny. This we have to face. Let destiny unfold, you just become the witness, the observer, and act with detachment."

I added, "If we 'know' that we always abide in the Truth, only then can we function with ease."

Swamiji replied, "You remain a sakshi and let it play out. It is better to be as an observer."

I answered, "Yes, we still have vasanas and cannot just give up everything."

He responded, "It is destiny, let it come. Who is functioning? This also is self-pride or ego. Let go, that's all."

I sat quietly trying to digest Swamiji's words. His presence inspired me to slide into a meditative mood; all surroundings forgotten.

Swamiji explained the sacred *Gayatri Mantra* to me. This is one of the most powerful mantras in the ancient *Rig Veda*:

Om bhur bhuwah swaha
Tat saviturvareniyam
Bhargo devasyadhi mahi
Dhiyo yonah pracho dayat

We meditate upon the auspicious
Godly Light of Lord Sun.
May that heavenly light illumine
the thought flow in our intellect

In Sanskrit *Gayatri* means *gayantam trayate iti Gayatri*, or the mantra which protects him who chants it. Orthodox priests believe it cannot be chanted by women and should be recited only at dawn, but Swamiji said I could do it any time before sunrise, before the sense perceptions arise. The ancient Hindu book of law *Manusmriti*, says, "In the early morning, by doing this japa in a standing position, one ends all sins committed during night. By doing japa in the evening in a sitting position, one ends one's sins committed during the day."

Swamiji also explained *diksha* (initiation). "It means a discipline which one undergoes in order that one may become fit for taking part in vedic ritual." Diksha is of various types, through the guru's sight, touch, word, mind, or through silence. The purpose of this is to purify the disciple or student and help his spiritual advancement.

I asked Swamiji, "Isn't it tragic, or is it our strong prarabdha, that even after knowing that one should spend maximum time with you, we still cannot remain with you Swamiji? So many people know you and yet they cannot see your *swaroopa* or true nature?"

Swamiji replied, "It is not easy to see the midday sun. One sees everything in its light but one cannot look directly at it because its light is blinding. You can see the rising and the setting sun but the midday sun can only be seen by one who is blind." By the latter he meant those who are blind to worldly existence.

We had this conversation when we were travelling by train. We could see our reflection in the glass window. Gradually, we could see the dawn's early light through that window. Then Swamiji said, "When there is a little light outside, both outside and inside are seen. When it is all light outside, then nothing inside can be seen, even though the light within is blazing."

While talking about prarabdha, Swamiji looked at me and said, "Who wanted all this?"

I replied, "Yes, that's true, so now nothing can be done till the next life?"

Swamiji shot back, "Why not? Here, even in this life, it may happen gradually. The light maybe lit within." I prayed silently, "Please make your words come true."

It was bliss, to sit quietly at his feet.

FEBRUARY 7, 1975
LUCKNOW

My family and other devotees came to the railway station to welcome Swamiji with garlands made with roses. There was a lot of excitement because this was the first Geeta Gyana Yagna in Lucknow by Swamiji.

Mohini and Chandra, Swamiji's long time devotees, came from Bombay to attend the yagna. In preparation we practiced chanting the Geeta chapter XII, which was the text selected for this yagna. In the evening, the venue was packed. Everyone chanted the *Guru Stotra*, a song in praise of the guru. The Governor of the State, Dr. M. Chenna Reddy, inaugurated the yagna. Mr. P.N. Chaturvedi, the chairman of the yagna committee, welcomed Swamiji and hailed him as the Vivekananda of the era. Swami Vivekananda was responsible for the revival of Hinduism in India. He was known for spreading Vedanta in the West and delivered his famous speech at the Parliament of World's Religions in Chicago in 1893.

The people were thrilled to hear our ancient Geeta explained in English. The satsangs in our home became a regular feature during Swamiji's stay. One day a *shastri* (scholar of Sanskrit) came to meet Swamiji. He had admired the discourse but was upset that Swamiji had delivered it in

English. Many orthodox scholars feel that our ancient scriptures should only be expounded in Hindi. Swamiji spoke to him in broken Hindi, "Shastriji, the Lord has a variety of *astra* and *shastra* (instruments and weapons). I am his astra to kill [the ego of] the English speaking people. In the present time many of our intelligent Hindus have settled overseas. They and their children need to be reminded of our ancient knowledge and culture. Even here in India many people are familiar with English. Hence the Lord has chosen 'this instrument' to do his work," said Swamiji, pointing to himself.

A few family members and friends stepped forward to help with the yagna. Unlike Bombay, Lucknow was a small city and I felt that the arrangements were not up to standard. Our home, though spacious, was simple and I kept feeling that we were not able to provide Swamiji with the comforts he deserved. Not too many from the business community attended the yagna. The donations collected on the final day were meager. While serving tea to Swamiji my eyes welled with tears as I expressed my disappointment. He lovingly said, "Shut up! I have not come here for comfort or for money but for your devotion. I was educated here in Lucknow and I wish to give back to this city whatever I can."

Swamiji continued to shower his special grace on our city of Lucknow by visiting it every year until 1992.

February 19, 1975
Powai Ashram

*I*T WAS A MOMENTOUS OCCASION. The *kumbhabhishekam* (consecration) ceremony of the Jagadeeshwara Shiva Temple took place on this day. Little did we realize the great honor Swamiji bestowed upon Ravindra and myself when he chose us to be the *yajman* (sponsor) of the event. As instructed by him we arrived at the temple in the early morning, dressed in traditional clothes which were bought specially for this occasion. The yajman is responsible for holding the intention for the puja being performed. We simply carried out Swamiji's sankalpa, the intention of *vishwa kalyana* or welfare of the universe. Starting with a *Ganapati Homa*, a prayer to Lord Ganesh, we performed the various rituals with a heart full of devotion. The energy was electric, and the sound of the mantras reverberated throughout the temple. Swamiji arrived under a ceremonial umbrella, led in a majestic procession with priests and brahmacharis reciting the vedas. They carried brass and copper urns filled with sacred Ganga water on their head. The *shikhar* (temple steeple) was washed with this water and the *kalasha* (brass pot) was installed by the resident *acharya* (teacher) Swami Dayananda.

We were overwhelmed when Hanumant Rao, the manager of the ashram, commented that Swamiji, by blessing us with this rare opportunity, had enabled us to accrue great merit or *punya* in this lifetime.

When we offered to pay for the puja expenses we were told that Swamiji had said an unequivocal "No." We were merely his representatives and perhaps he did not want us to increase our ego and vanity by performing this special ritual.

We received another gift from Swamiji when he gave us the privilege to donate three silver kalashas. I was totally taken aback when Swamiji himself accompanied me to Jhaveri Bazaar, the famous jewelry market in Bombay, to place the order for the urns. He personally selected the intricate design. They were filled with holy Ganga river water and ultimately installed beside the main statue of Lord Shiva in the Powai temple where they are worshipped even today.

June 15, 1975
Allentown, Pennsylvania

*O*nce again Swamiji was invited to Allentown by my sister Preeta and her husband Gopal. En route to Philadelphia for a talk, Gopal asked Swamiji about Satya Sai Baba who was known for performing miracles, "Why don't more people do the same? Can you also Swamiji?"

Swamiji replied, "Sai Baba of Shirdi did many miracles. He said no one came to get the real teaching." He added, "I am serving those who have awakened, not the masses. I will consider it a wonderful success if even ten disciples will emerge, who will hold the masses around them. As for Satya Sai Baba if he performed miracles on a platform, what would you call it? Magic? It becomes divine because he is doing it. There are *siddhis* (super natural powers gained through rigorous penance) and many seekers acquire them while on the spiritual path. As the mind becomes meditative and quiet, its powers increase. Even a genius doesn't express the total potential of the mind. Some seekers stop seeking after they achieve siddhis. They gradually develop an ego and start performing miracles. After this ego is developed the mind becomes agitated and the powers diminish."

Swamiji continued, "Many people become utterly selfish. They can neither grow nor become intellectual so, for them, such miracles are good. It makes them believe there is a God. When the miracle performer tells them I can do so because I pray to God, then they also start praying to God."

Another question was posed, "Swamiji, ninety percent of the people are like that, so why don't more teachers perform miracles?"

Swamiji replied, "It may be good in the beginning but later on, when the mind is more mature, it requires knowledge of the truth. For example, nursery school is all right in the beginning, but later on you need a college education."

Gopal again asked Swamiji, "Meditation is becoming very popular these days, what do you think?"

Swamiji replied, "Without knowing and fixing a purpose or goal these days people plan to do instant meditation. I want to correct that thinking. All Masters took a long time: Christ, Buddha, Muhammad. Great care should be taken. Preparation for meditation is very important."

Gopal asked, "Why is the repetition of mantra done?"

Swamiji's reply was very concise, "To tame the mind! If you want to tame the mind you should first know what the mind is." Swamiji explained, "Mind is thought flow. Just as water flowing continuously towards one direction is called a stream or a river, in the same way, thought flow is called the mind."

Swamiji quoted in Sanskrit, "*Sankalpdhara manah*" (thought flow is mind). The taming of the mind is done in the same way as taming a river. We can divert the flow in three ways." He then elaborated on the three paths of yoga.

The first is through changing the quality of thought which is done through bhakti yoga (devotion and surrender). The second is changing the quantity of thought which is done through karma yoga. The third is changing the direction of the thought flow which is achieved through gyana yoga (knowledge).

Swamiji concluded by saying, "These efforts create the difference between remaining a *bhogi* (sensual person) or becoming a *yogi* (spiritual person). The past, present and future are the three sources of flooding the mind. If the river is dried up the river bed is evident. In the same manner when the thoughts are quiet then the substratum of thought, which is Consciousness, is self-evident."

JUNE 16, 1975
ALLENTOWN, PENNSYLVANIA

ONE DAY WHILE GOING DOWN the stairs I fell and hurt myself. I had been feeling homesick and was missing my children and in that vulnerable state I burst into tears. A thought crossed my mind that perhaps my karma was being taken care of by experiencing some bearable physical and emotional pain in the presence of my Guru.

June 21, 1975
Satsang

*D*uring satsang Swamiji was asked many questions. His responses were brief and tailored to the seeker who was looking for simple answers to help with his spiritual practice. Some of these answers are reproduced below.

On Reincarnation:

"It is an assumption of Hinduism. Religion must be supported by a philosophy which logically explains what is seen and experienced by an individual and how it relates to the higher reality. When disparities in life do not arise from any visible cause, they must be the effect of some invisible past causes. Thus, we arrive at the theory of reincarnation which says that we are products of all our past experience (including past lives). One cannot remember the past life; however, you can just look for the pattern in your present life. That is enough."

On Atheists:

"Those denying God are only denying their own misconception of what God is. Some investigation into that which you are denying is necessary or the denial proves useless.

The word God is only a sound. What does this sound symbolize? That is what one must investigate for oneself. God is Truth. God is that which remains constant in the past, present and the future. All else is false."

On our relationship with God according to Hinduism:

"This idea of God as sitting and running the show is a poetic point of view. It has no philosophical support. The Creator endows us with the mental and physical equipment, which is our mind and body. He also presents the situations in our life according to our own blueprint; so that we can exhaust our unfulfilled desires.

"The three well known Hindu philosophers [from the 8th to the 13th century] accept the Upanishads as authority and the existence of the 'One Absolute Reality'. They agree that the goal of life is God-realization and not just experiences in this finite world. They differ in the relationship between the individual and the Divine.

"Sri Madhava, the dualist, says that you are eternally separate from the Divine. He is correct from his point of view. When one is identified with the body, one is eternally separate from God.

"Sri Ramanuja claims that you are an aspect of God. You are a drop in the ocean, but you can never know the ocean. He too is accurate from his vantage point. When one is identified with one's mind, one is a part of the whole.

"Adi Shankaracharya, the preceptor of Advaita Vedanta, declares that in your essence you are identical with the One (God). According to him, you are the eternal, essential divinity, transcending both the physical and emotional instruments.

"These great teachers are all correct because your relationship with God depends on your point of view. When you are standing on a mountain peak, looking down at the temple in the valley, you are separate from that temple. When you go down from that mountain and enter into the temple gates, you become a part of the temple complex. However, when you enter the sanctum sanctorum, you and the Lord of the temple are one. All three philosophers are defining your relationship to God. The relationship may change, but God remains the same."

June 21, 1975
Evening Discourse

*I*n the car on the way back from the evening talk, Swamiji started to tell us about the future *Avatar*, Kali. He is supposed to be the tenth and last incarnation of Lord Vishnu during this *Kali Yuga*. This is a period in the history of mankind when the dark forces of nature become very active and there is a total breakdown of morals and values. Swamiji said, "I have come to prepare for him."

June 22, 1975

*I*n the morning when I took Swamiji his tea, he gave me a letter to read. It was from a prisoner who had been indicted on a marijuana charge. He had requested some books on Vedanta. Swamiji said, "He seems a very sincere seeker." I felt touched and thought how impartial a true teacher is in helping seekers from all over the globe, even reaching out to those in prison.

During the evening discourses on the Geeta Swamiji said, "In nature, the creative process is always slow. Whenever there is rush and force there is destruction. For example, compare a soft gentle breeze to a gale. Evolution happens slowly, like a sunrise. Vedanta philosophy is about evolution not revolution." Swamiji's comments during satsang made us pause and contemplate.

"Solutions are never given by the teacher. The problem should be cleared by you, through your thinking. The flower must come from the tree, not the gardener. We can only provide nourishment, like the gardener nourishes the plant by improving the soil, water, etc."

Function of a master after realization:

"The entire universe is like a web, interconnected. Each individual is a 'subject' and with reference to himself, all other people and things are 'objects'. Everyone's vasanas affect the other. The individual has microcosmic vasanas, while the totality has macrocosmic vasanas. It is like the national debt and the personal debt. In the same way, I created my personal vasanas and through the three yogas I exhausted my personal vasanas, but not the universal vasanas. After realization, the total demand, total vasanas [which are called collective consciousness] are still functioning through a realized master."

June 25, 1975
Montreal, Canada

*I*n the morning, I served tea to Swamiji and Reverend Elizabeth Burrows. She had arrived from Seattle the previous night. They were engaged in a very interesting conversation. The Reverend was telling Swamiji about her mystical experiences. Swamiji responded, "Reject them and go beyond; drop it."

She asked Swamiji about conflict between the mind and intellect, good and evil and of the struggle within.

Swamiji answered, "Go beyond both, to the Father in Heaven. Ramkrishna Paramhansa and his disciple Swami Vivekananda also felt the struggle within."

The Reverend complained about too many mystical experiences, voices and visions. Swamiji told her, "They will be helpful in communicating with and understanding other students' problems. Some masters just get into the transcendental experience but they cannot understand the seeker's viewpoint; that's why the seeker cannot comprehend that which is beyond the mind. Such a guru chisels words but cannot come down to the level of the average student. Those who have had 'It' [self-realization], know that they have had 'It.'"

Swamiji added, "Our Eastern philosophy is called a darshan or vision. It is not a mere 'view', but a way of 'life' which can be directly experienced."

June 28, 1975
Montreal, Canada
Lunch bhiksha at Mr. Bali's house

Swamiji stressed the importance of selfless service on the path of spirituality. He emphasized that even for material progress society needs to be less self-centred on the individual. He then narrated the story of *Bending the Elbow*.

"Before coming on this trip, I [Swamiji] decided to peep in the heavens and meet God. He hosted a banquet in order to distribute nectar to all the demons and angels. The angels complained. Why is God inviting the demons too? God replied that for him everyone is the same and they could all have their fill of nectar. However, there was one condition. They had to eat without bending their elbows. The demons got very angry saying that this was a trick; how could one eat this way? They all walked out protesting. The angels, having faith in God, kept sitting. I waited to see what they would do. Would they eat like animals on all fours? Then I saw each angel feeding the other without bending the elbow. How did they do this? They extended their arm to feed the person seated next to them without bending the elbow. With this mutual exchange they were able to fulfill God's condition. The Lord gives us plenty but we become absolutely selfish and neither leave, like the demons, nor help and feed the other, but break the law by bending the elbow and then suffer. The elbow can be bent only in one direction, towards oneself; it denotes ego and selfishness. Keep the arm and elbow straight, it will always point out towards God, or our fellow beings. The attitude should be: all is His glory not mine; only then can we drink the nectar of life."

Dinner bhiksha at Mr G.P. Khare's house

Mr Khare was a devotee of the great master Sri Aurobindo of Pondicherry. He had invited many guests and several of them asked questions which I found helpful in my own spiritual quest.

Regarding *prarabdha* (destiny) and *purushartha* (self-effort, free will) Swamiji said, "What you meet in life as a result of your past actions is prarabdha. How you meet it, is purushartha. Free will is not total freedom to act, in as much as one cannot order all circumstances and situations in life to suit one's own liking. But in any given situation, the person is free to decide how to react to it; to choose her mental attitude towards it and decide how she should deal with it; all this is her purushartha.

"The mental *bhava* (mood) involves keeping a positive attitude and maintaining the balance of mind in sorrow or happiness, victory or defeat. This is the self-effort or free will to be exercised by the seeker. However, the material results of this self effort or purushartha are influenced by the destiny of each individual.

"*Yoga Vashishta*, Bhagavad Geeta, and many other sacred books praise self-effort. For achieving success, they advise the spiritual seeker persist in *vichar* (reflection) and *abhyas* (practice)."

June 29, 1975
Ottawa, Canada

There are many different ways that one learns from a master. Attending discourses, watching videos and listening to audios of the teachings are all very valuable. However, nothing compares to just sitting in the presence of a master and receiving spontaneous teaching when he is in an exalted mood. One such satsang took place after breakfast when a close circle of devotees sat at the feet of Swamiji. He established a rapport with each person and the questions and answers flowed, transporting us into a state of heightened awareness.

Question: "Please explain the Supramental mind?"
Answer: "*Sattwic manas, sattwaguna pradhan manaha,* (the peaceful, intelligent, alert mind) is the highest state of mind. The seeker needs to remain steady in this state and when one reaches there, automatically one glides into the Reality."

Question: "After receiving the knowledge from the guru, why doesn't a person 'realize'?"
Answer: "If he is a true guru he will give the reason to those seekers who have merely understood the reality intellectually. The layer of vasanas [impressions] within us is the main reason for not 'realizing.' The guru explains how to remove them through the three yogas of karma, bhakti and gyana. One main path in Vedanta is gyana yoga or the path of knowledge, which also involves deep meditation. It is practiced after mental purification or practiced along with karma and bhakti yoga."

In response to a question, Swamiji touched upon the concept of sin. "Sin means any act which is self-insulting, which agitates the mind and intellect of the doer. An act that may be a sin for one person may not be a sin for another, depending on their samskaras or cultural upbringing and sensitivity. For example a Westerner eating meat since childhood is not committing a sin, but an orthodox Hindu Brahmin who starts eating meat just to conform to society may be committing a sin."

Question: "What is doubt?"
Answer: "It is a gap in our understanding. When a new idea is presented to us, our intellect finds it to be logical. However, our own prior experience does not allow us to accept the idea completely; giving rise to a doubt. A bridge is to be built for clearing the doubt. Through the correct thought process the mind integrates the two ideas thereby creating a new understanding."

Question: "What are the different alternative planes of consciousness, till the experience of Reality?"
Answer: "Like from waking to deep sleep, there are various planes of consciousness."

Question: "Is Cosmic Consciousness an egoless state?"
Answer: "Yes, I would consider it so."

June 30, 1975
Val-Morin, Quebec, Canada
Meeting with Swami Vishnudevananda

*A*fter the evening lecture I accompanied Swamiji to the Sivananda Yoga Ashram in Laurentia at the invitation of Swami Vishnudevananda. Located in the Val-Morin hills about fifty miles from Montreal, it is a quiet retreat for those primarily interested in *hatha* yoga. Both Swamis had received their initiation in 1949 by Swami Sivananda at his ashram in Rishikesh and were spiritual brothers.

In Val-Morin Swamiji gave a talk to the yoga teacher trainees on the topic *Infinite Temple of Reality*. He elaborated on this by quoting from the Upanishads, "*Tapah, Damah, Karmiti, Pratishta, Satya ayatanah*" and suggested that these words represent the 'temple' each seeker must build for herself. *Tapah* is austerity, *Damah* is control of the senses, *Karma* is selfless action. These are the foundations for yoga and they are protected by *Satya*, the Truth.

Later in the evening Swamiji asked me to remain in the room while both Swamis had their bhiksha. As they conversed over dinner Swami Vishnudevananda said, "Swamiji you are the greatest living Vedantin in the world." Swamiji just smiled.

Swami Vishnudevananda continued, "Why don't you come and stay here. I will renew your heart through hatha yoga. You need to rest. I will overhaul your system, then you can go on serving all mankind."

Swamiji smiled and replied, "Who wants to get a new heart? No one can go on serving everyone forever." Pointing towards his body, Swamiji continued, "This is an old machine. No spare parts are available. I don't want it to go to the junkyard to be recycled. I will remove the license plate and dump it in another state."

There is a deep meaning in these words as they refer to the state of liberation.

JULY 1, 1975
ALLENTOWN, PENNSYLVANIA, USA

Swamiji left Canada and returned to the United States to continue his lecture series. I was scheduled to go back to India. This led to a conversation whether a disciple should be staying near, or far away from the guru. Swamiji mentioned the example of bouncing a ball. He said, "When you feel down or you are far away from me, I am actually lifting you up. If one wants to go higher there has to be separation for some time."

Swamiji started to pack his suitcase. During those days he did his packing himself. In later years he gave his close disciples the opportunity to serve him and perform these tasks. He pulled out a bottle of vitamin E capsules and handed them to me saying, "Go and give this to Swami Akhandanandaji in India. Convey *Om Namo Narayanaya* [a greeting used by monks when meeting each other] from me and say Swami Chinmayananda has sent this for you."

Swami Akhandananda was one of the most revered Sanskrit scholars and famous for his discourses on the Shrimad Bhagvatam. This is a classic piece of literature which expounds the acme of devotion as well as the deeper truths of Vedanta. I was finally able to meet him in Bombay and had the good fortune to attend many of his talks. He and Swamiji had a very good rapport and I felt that they shone like one light and blessed our entire family in the years to come. Swamiji became our family guru and my sister Rashmi's family accepted Swami Akhandanandaji as their guru.

Swami Chinmayananda is like the blazing sun that rises from the banks of the Ganga, making everyone see the reality through the light of knowledge. Swami Akhandananda Maharaj is like the cool moon that rises from the banks of the river Yamuna, nourishing one and all, with the nectar of bhakti or devotion. At this stage of my life these two teachers provided me with the right environment to ripen the seed of awareness sown by Swamiji.

Two great masters at our home. Swamiji and
Swami Akhandanandaji Maharaj. Bombay, 17 January, 1977

The spiritual master Meher Baba once said,

"The grace of the God Man is like the rain, which falls equally on all lands irrespective of whether they are barren or fertile; but it fructifies only in the lands that have been rendered fertile through arduous and patient toiling."[1]

The role of the guru is to make his disciples think clearly and freely, and to help them understand the mysteries of themselves and the world. His words are only part of his teachings; his presence alone is his most powerful tool. Though he does not transform his disciples all at once into spiritual giants, his life and teachings have a lasting influence on their evolving minds. As Swamiji said, "The *Sadguru* and the seeker have a relationless relationship."

A new chapter was waiting to be written as I continued my spiritual journey towards equanimity and harmony within the Self and all around me!

Hari Om!

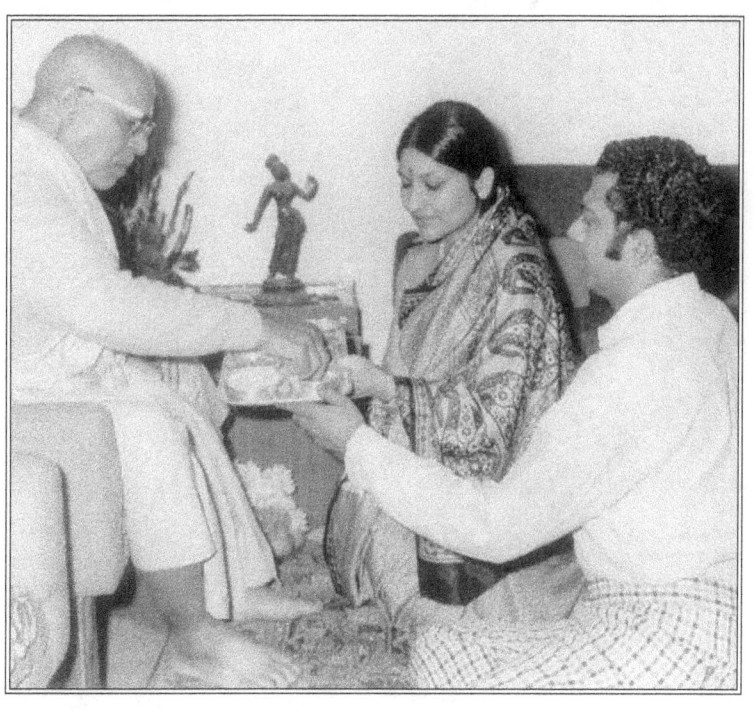

Offering dry fruit to Swami Akhandanandaji Maharaj,
17 January, 1977

Swamiji feeding me. Sidhabari, 1987

Epilogue

*'The heart would have no rainbow,
if the eyes had no tears.'*

These words were printed on a card that Swami Chinmayananda presented to me in April 1976 while we were in Jaipur. As he handed me the card Swamiji said, "Now your period of tears starts." At that time I had no idea of the gravity of those words and what they would mean in my life.

During the early years of my study and travel with Swamiji, from 1973 to 1975, my entire spiritual focus was on seeking my true Self. Every action of mine was dedicated to that goal. In a letter that Swamiji wrote to me in March 1973, he enunciated the quality of a seeker who pursues his goal with total devotion "... *When you take up to a thing you know, no half-way course, you go at it fully, entirely, totally with everything you have in you. This is a rare dynamic way of life. Nothing half hearted, hesitating, about your actions. This is good for sadhaks.*"

By God's grace, from the moment that I first met Swamiji, I felt intuitively that he was God-like or, in modern terminology, a man of perfection. This feeling became even stronger after I visited Uttarkashi with him for the first time. Later, I read that a disciple should have the same devotion for her guru as she does for God and consider them as one. Sri Adi Shankaracharya's foremost disciple, Sureshwaracharya, wrote a commentary on his revered teacher's poem, *Hymn to Dakshinamurti*. In his conclusion he quotes from a famous Upanishad which echoes this belief:

> *Yasya deve paraa bhaktih yathaa deve tathaa gurau,*
> *tasyaite kathitaa hyarthaah prakaashante mahaatmanah*

The one who has supreme devotion to the Lord and the same devotion to the guru, to him alone the meaning of these words (scriptures) becomes extremely clear.

When he signed my membership form for the Chinmaya Mission Swamiji said, "You may become a member, but let me warn you that in the spiritual path you are alone. The ashram or Mission activities may help initially to purify your heart by working in a yagna spirit of karma yoga, but it has limitations. To realize the highest goal you have to walk the path alone." He told me, "I am not appointing you as a Trustee of the Chinmaya Mission Trusts. Even without any position in the organization, whatever work you do for me or the Mission, consider it as an offering to the Lord, done with selfless devotion. This will really help in your spiritual unfoldment."

During 1976 to 1983, I went through an extremely difficult time personally. I overcame some health issues which were followed by a deep joy in the birth of our youngest child, our daughter Shreya. Soon after, major problems surfaced in our family business and my husband's health declined. All of this caused financial difficulties. This was a turbulent period for us, especially for my husband who went into a deep depression. The changing attitudes of our extended family and friends and their indifference to our problems, came as a great shock.

Because of these challenging circumstances, we were unable to be with Swamiji as much as we would have liked. During one of his unexpected visits to our home in December 1979, Swamiji told me to remember his words, "Whatever happens, consider all this like a dream. Your true Self is the witness. The light within is unattached, unaffected, eternally pure. You hold on to this light which will enable you to retain the balance of your mind and keep you calm."

The words from Swamiji's Geeta lessons echoed in my mind, "*Samattwam yoga uchyate*", balance of mind is yoga.

It was Swamiji's Grace that even in these difficult days we were blessed by the visits and teachings of the great Masters Sri Nisargadutta Maharaj, Swami Akhandandaji and. It seems as if our spiritual family doctor, Swamiji, was sending us for necessary treatment to specialists in the diseases of the ego and its samsara.

These holistic treatments by various spiritual methods contributed towards us regaining a healthy and balanced personality.

Sometimes the guru will test the disciple's loyalty to the goal, the highest truth, rather than towards the teacher. It is possible that Swamiji was sending me to different masters for this purpose, so that I might see the essence of truth that lies within all masters regardless of their method of teaching.

From 1984 to 1996, Swamiji's protective grace and perfect guidance cushioned the violent upheaval in our lives and we gradually attuned ourselves to the daily rhythms of ordinary life. I was no longer affected by the outward swings of life and was now able to face them relatively calmly.

My education which included a Bachelors degree in Law had qualified me to pursue a career. I found the courage again to face the world and start participating in new roles. So far I had just been a wife and mother, a homemaker. I now began to get involved in my husband's small business. I also coordinated research in the manufacture of herbal health and beauty products which were based on the Indian traditional medicine, *Ayurveda*. This was a business that I grew on my own, and it was a proud day when I started to export my products to an overseas market. I had complete faith in these formulations because I had used them personally.

With such a busy schedule my work became my prayer. But my foremost duty was being a mother. My husband and I worked very hard to provide the best possible education for our children. With all the experience I had gained, I was able to serve as a trustee in various social welfare organizations, as well as become a director in a bank. For me this was a period of dynamic activity, referred to as *rajasic* activity in Vedanta.

Swamiji's Mahasamadhi in 1993 brought on a gradual change in my rajasic behavior. For a true seeker a master's passing away brings the disciple closer to the essence of his being. Even though I missed his physical presence he had always taught us to go beyond the framework of the body. In the months to follow I felt his presence within my heart even more. Although nothing can compare to the actual moments I spent with Swamiji, they crystallised as vivid memories within me and I began to feel as if there was no separation between us. My mind quietened and I became more peaceful and steady *(sattwic)*. I wanted to spend time in japa, pilgrimage and swadhyaya.

My mind constantly wanted to reflect on the teachings of the Upanishads and holy texts such as the Bhagavad Geeta, Ramayana, Srimad Bhagavatam and Yoga Vashishta. I was hungry for knowledge about the lives of the various seekers (*bhaktas*), saints and masters and wanted to participate in satsangs with their disciples. I also visited other spiritual teachers whenever the opportunity arose.

In recent years my life seems more settled. The turbulence of the past appears like a distant dream. Of course there are always challenges to be met and problems to be faced, but the spark of light that Swamiji lit within me is always present. I feel it deeply. The spiritual seeker in me knows that in response to my prayer it is the ever compassionate Lord who comes to bless, in the form of a guru.

I offer my salutations to Swamiji and other spiritual teachers, who function in the world by spreading their light of knowledge. Sri Shankaracharya's text Vivekachoodamani sums it up beautifully in verse 578:

His mind immersed in the ocean of eternal bliss, forever wandering about, indeed blessing the whole world.

Walking with Windows of Light is a glimpse of the spiritual gift I received from Swamiji and the other Masters. As I continue to walk my journey, I am grateful for these blessings that have allowed me to share my story with you.

Extended family and Chinmaya devotees with Swamiji. Swami Tejomayananda is 4th from the right. Ahmedabad, 1978

My family with Swamiji in our Lucknow home 1987. My mother Swarnlata Tandon is seated behind Swamiji. The portrait is of my father Prem Narain Tandon.

Notes

January 7, 1973
Sandeepany Sadhanalaya Ashram
Powai, Bombay

1. Swami Chinmayananda, *Self Unfoldment* (Mumbai, India: Central Chinmaya Mission Trust, 2007), 41.

March 1973
Uttarkashi

1. Munagala Venkataramiah, *Talks with Sri Ramana Maharshi* (Tiruvannamalai, India: Sri Ramanasramam, 2010) - Talk no. 275.

July 1, 1975
Allentown, Pennsylvania, USA

1. Meher Baba, *Discourses* (Ahmednagar, India: Avatar Meher Baba Perpetual Public Charitable Trust, 1987), 286-287.

MAY 6, 1973
NATIONAL GEETA GYANA YAGNA
BANGALORE

1. Swami Chinmayananda, *The Holy Geeta* (Mumbai, India: Central Chinmaya Mission Trust).

CHAPTER #	VERSE #
II	47, 48
III	21, 30
IV	24
VI	5, 24
IX	4, 18, 21, 22, 26
X	41
XI	41
XII	54, 55
XIII	2, 6, 7, 8, 12
XV	5, 12, 14, 15
XVIII	45, 46, 47, 65, 66

Author Bio

Neeru Mehta grew up in Lucknow, India in a socially and culturally vibrant family. She excelled in academics and won the Chancellor's Silver Medal when she graduated from Lucknow University with a degree in Bachelor of Arts. Later she pursued a degree in law and went on to win the Chancellor's Gold medal. Neeru established a herbal cosmetic business, served on the board of Andhra Bank and was the Chairperson of the Gujarat Chamber of Commerce's women's wing. She resides in Ahmedabad with her husband and is a proud grandmother of three. She has also written *Swamin Namaste* in Hindi and published Swamiji's handwritten notes, *Scraps & Bits*. Neeru continues to pursue her spiritual life as an avid vedantin. Swami Chinmayananda and other masters remain her guiding light even today.

Editorial Team: Deborah Seroff, Poonam Patni, Rajpriya, and Shubhraji

For more info:
www.WalkingWithWindowsofLight.com
www.namahom.org

www.ingramcontent.com/pod-product-compliance
Lightning Source LLC
Chambersburg PA
CBHW022114040426
42450CB00006B/697